Teen Feng Shui

Design Your Space, Design Your Life

SUSAN LEVITT

Bindu Books

Rochester, Vermont

Bindu Books
One Park Street
Rochester, Vermont 05767
www.InnerTraditions.com

Bindu Books is a division of Inner Traditions International

Library of Congress Cataloging-in-Publication Data

Levitt, Susan.
  Teen feng shui : design your space, design your life / Susan Levitt.
     p. cm.
  ISBN 0-89281-916-2 (pbk.)
 1. Feng shui. 2. Taoism. 3. Teenagers. I. Title: Design your space, design your life. 1971- III. Title.

BF1779.F4L465 2003
133.3′337—dc21
                              2003000745

Printed and bound in the United States at Lake Book Manufacturing, Inc.

10 9 8 7 6 5 4 3 2 1

Text design and layout by Priscilla Baker
This book was typeset in Legacy Serif Book with Calligraphic as a display typeface

Contents

Introduction

Finding My Path

was age seventeen when I found the world of Chinese culture—a discovery that completely changed the course of my life. All I knew about Chinese culture before that were the kung fu movies of Bruce Lee. I also was seventeen when I started college in Chicago, but I didn't know what to major in or what classes to take. So I looked through all the books in the university bookstore to see what might be interesting.

One book, *Temple of the Golden Pavilion,* caught my eye. It was about a teen who was also trying to find his place in the world and to fit in. The book was for a class called Japanese Literature. I had no idea what that was, but I took the class because I liked the book. The class professor, Dr. Takeko Stover, was the best teacher I ever had. I ended up taking all her classes: Chinese Literature, Chinese History, Japanese History, and Asian Art History. Before I knew it, I was an Asian Studies major.

All my friends thought this was really weird. How would this prepare me for a real job? And how could I major in Asian Studies when I'm not even Asian? And what was Asian Studies anyway? But I knew I was on to something that I loved and found fascinating, so I pursued it. I took a Chinese calligraphy class at The School of the Art Institute of Chicago and completed my education there with a degree in fine art.

I then moved to San Francisco to study traditional Chinese medicine. I had experienced major health problems that were cured through Chinese medicine, mostly by using acupuncture—where fine needles are inserted into energy points of the body—and by drinking brews made from Chinese herbs. As I learned more about Chinese medicine, I also learned about feng shui, the Chinese art of placement. To stay healthy, one must live and sleep in a balanced environment. I had lived in such negative and chaotic environments in Chicago that it was no wonder I was always sick and couldn't get better. And with my art training, I knew how color and design could make a beautiful living space. I really took to feng shui.

Feng shui and Chinese medicine saved my life. I was not on a deathbed, but spiritually I was a lost soul. Now I enjoy excellent health, walk a spiritual path, have a philosophy for life, and know how to create peace, compassion, and contentment for myself and others. I work as a spiritual counselor and also do feng shui for people's homes and offices.

As you read the pages of this book, you too will be embarking on a new journey of self-knowledge, discovery, and transformation. You can design your room to create whatever you want in life. This is the feng shui book I wish I had when I was a teen. May it inspire you to follow your own interests, listen to your truth, and find great joy.

Part One

The Magic
of Feng Shui

ave you ever walked into a friend's house and felt immediately comfortable and relaxed? Or have you walked into a room or building and suddenly felt restless and agitated? If you've ever experienced a spontaneous response when entering a new space, you have been affected by feng shui.

Whether or not you are aware of it, every space you walk into influences your emotions and behavior, and the emotions and behavior of the people around you. Just as a stone at the bottom of a river will influence the current of the water, the way objects are placed within a space will influence the people and energies that circulate around that object. For more than five thousand years people have been designing spaces according to feng shui, the Chinese art of placement. Correct feng shui encourages people and the invisible energies around them to behave in a way that will attract knowledge, health, fame, helping hands, a successful career, fortune, and romance.

This book gives you the basic tools you'll need to practice feng shui in your room, and your life, as you see fit. You can use feng shui to make your living space more creative, more relaxing, more social, more inviting, and more in harmony with who you are and who you want to be. Most feng shui books are for adults, who use feng shui to design an entire house or workplace. This book is just for teens and is based on the fact that most of you have only one or two rooms under your immediate control. So, the focus of this book will be on your bedroom or dorm room as the primary

4

place where you sleep, work, create, communicate, relax, exercise, and live your private, independent life. Here's how this book works:

The first part explains where feng shui comes from, why it works, and how it can work for you. It also explains the hands-on tools you will need to do feng shui.

The second part tells you how to apply these tools and gets you started with redesigning your room. In this part you'll learn where to put the larger items in your room.

In part 3 you can decide what you want to attract in your life—everything from love to fame to peace in your family. You can refine the feng shui arrangement of the items in your room to support your goals.

In the fourth, and final, part of the book you'll learn how to increase the power of your room through the use of feng shui cures, astrology, and five Chinese elements.

Feng shui can sometimes seem a bit complicated. It can be challenging to work with invisible forces and find creative ways to apply an ancient Chinese practice to your contemporary room. As you try out the different techniques in this book, I recommend the following tips:

◉ **Be brave.** If you want big changes in your life, make big changes in your room. Stretching beyond the familiar is a great way to discover new parts of yourself and invite new, exciting energy into your life. Anything you change today can be changed again tomorrow, so there's no reason not to take risks. Use the principles of feng shui to make changes and then watch what happens, perhaps using notes or a journal as a way to look closely at the results.

◉ **Be creative.** Feng shui can apply to any space, from a mansion to a cardboard box. Use your creativity to interpret how feng shui might apply to your specific situation and the rooms of friends and family members.

☯ **Trust your intuition.** If something doesn't feel right about a certain feng shui suggestion when it's applied to your room, don't do it. Though it can often take awhile to understand and describe the energies at work around us, we can often instinctively sense whether something feels "right" or if something feels a little "off." Trust your own intuition in finding arrangements that work for you.

☯ **Don't take my word for it.** The tools in this book should give you everything you need to do feng shui in your own room. But there are many additional resources and schools out there to help you develop and advance your understanding of feng shui and the Taoist spirituality from which it was born. Pay attention to your own experiences and budding interests as you go and don't be afraid to seek out additional teachers to feed the fires of your curiosity.

☯ **Enjoy yourself.** Even though feng shui is very ancient knowledge, you can use it in a playful spirit: do feng shui with friends, do feng shui to your favorite music, or do feng shui speaking out loud in the accent of your favorite imagined interior decorator. Whatever your pleasure, have fun with feng shui.

1

Feng What?

eng shui (pronounced "fung schway") is known as "the Chinese art of placement." It is an ancient Chinese science that tells us how to build our human environment—from rooms to houses to towns—in accordance with the forces of nature. When we do this, we harness the capacity to attract the things we want, whether it be wealth, romance, or good friends.

Chances are you have used feng shui in your life and not even known it. Picture this: You're at the beach and you're looking for a place to set down your towel. You look at the position of your towel in relation to the sun, the ocean, and other people around you. You move a few rocks out of the way so you're more comfortable when you lay down. Or perhaps you are entering a subway car or bus and scan the available seats to decide where you want to sit, before choosing one that just "feels right." Consciously or not, you choose to place yourself and your stuff in a way that enhances your experience of the surrounding environment. Feng shui does the same thing.

The science of feng shui is based on knowledge that is over 5,000 years old. It represents generations of observations about the way the natural world moves and shifts. Based on these observations, feng shui tells us how to position ourselves and our things in ways that maximize our comfort and create balance in the world.

Feng = Wind

Shui = Water

The Chinese words *feng* and *shui* literally translate to "wind" and "water." Wind represents the movement or flow called universal forces through the central life force called *chi* (we'll be looking more closely at chi in chapter 2). Water also moves and flows; it can be a tiny trickle or a huge crashing wave. Wind can be a tornado or a gentle breeze. When wind and water flow in balance things run smoothly. On a personal scale, this means our experience as individuals is comfortable and the things we aspire to and wish to attract come to us easily. On a universal scale, it means all things are in their naturally intended order. You can use the techniques of feng shui to design any environment: your room, dorm, desk, school locker, and other personal places. First, though, you'll need to familiarize yourself with some of the concepts that I'll be referring to throughout the book.

How It Works

Just as people have personalities, objects and colors have certain individual qualities. Every item that surrounds you represents some quality of the universe. Feng shui uses light, color, location, and object placement to create balance in your present and to influence the direction of your future. Feng shui will not only tell you where the best place for your posters may be, it will encourage you to look at how one thing in your room (say, for example, a lamp) interacts with all the other things in your room. Imagine a soccer coach preparing plays for an upcoming game. The coach will observe all of her players for various qualities such as speed, strength, ability to make fast decisions, interaction with other team members, and control over the soccer ball. The coach then uses her observations to figure out which team members go where, and what role they might have in the overall game. The coach might decide to place two players next to each other because they work well with each other, or she might decide to keep one player in a specific part of the field. With feng shui, you are that coach. Your stuff is the team you are arranging, and your room—or any other space you choose to feng shui—is your playing field. In the next few chapters, you will learn the rules of the game: how to interpret the spaces of your room, where to place your furniture, and how to observe characteristics of objects to come up with the "winning" combinations you are seeking.

Understanding relationships between objects can be difficult. Objects don't talk. It's not as if your tangerine computer is going to look at you and say, "I really can't stand that purple poster. I mean, every time we're together I feel like I've got to compete for your attention!" But you can understand a lot about the dynamics between objects based on their color,

ACTIVITY: TUNING IN TO PLACE

As you pay increasing attention to your environment and how you respond to it, you will grow to understand which characteristics influence chi. This is an easy exercise that you can do anywhere to help you develop the skill of "tuning in" to the spaces around you.

Directions: Fill out the chart on the following pages. Start with the left column. In the first three rows (1–3), write down your three favorite spaces (specific rooms, houses, parks, or buildings, for example). In the next three rows (4–6) write down your three least favorite spaces. Now move across the chart, completing the sentences at the top of each column with the first word or two that comes to your mind. Do this for each of the six places you have just listed.

TUNING IN TO PLACE

	I go to this place to . . .	When I'm in this place I feel . . .	The lighting in this place is . . .
Three of your favorite spaces			
1.			
2.			
3.			
Three of your least favorite spaces			
4.			
5.			
6.			

Take a moment to analyze your answers. What combinations of characteristics please you most? What combinations seem to displease you most? These questions will train you to become increasingly sensitive to the qualities that create an enjoyable environment as well as those you wish to avoid. As you read

The colors in this place are . . .	The materials used in this space are (wood, cement, brick) . . .	The smell of this place is . . .	The living things in this place are . . .	The thing I notice most about this place is . . .

through the pages of this book, you will be able to combine your newfound sensitivity to place with feng shui facts in order to create the most comfortable environments for yourself and others.

In harmony with the Tao,

the sky is clear and spacious,

the earth is solid and full,

all creatures flourish together,

content with the way they are,

endlessly repeating themselves,

endlessly renewed.

When man interferes with the Tao,

the sky becomes filthy,

the earth becomes depleted,

the equilibrium crumbles,

creatures become extinct.

The Master views the parts with
compassion,

because he understands the whole.

His constant practice is humility.

He doesn't glitter like a jewel

But lets himself be shaped by the Tao,

As rugged and common as stone.

—LAO-TZU, FROM THE *TAO TE CHING*

shape, and the material from which they are made. Then you can tap in to the 5,000 years of amassed knowledge of feng shui to know how those different characteristics are related to one another. In this way, you begin to see the bigger picture, the whole of your room, and understand the subtle relationships among objects enough to move things around to create a stronger environment. Each time you walk into your room you will be able to see an integrated expression of yourself, while simultaneously seeing all of the diverse parts of your life, hopes, and dreams that make you, you. And others who enter the room will see it too. You should feel at home in your room. Feng shui will help you do this.

Where Did Feng Shui Come From?

The ancient Chinese studied nature to make sense of the universe. They studied chi, the energy of life, and developed a spiritual worldview based on the balance of nature. This worldview became the philosophy of Taoism (pronounced "Dowism"). The priests of Taoism, who were both male and female, observed landforms, river flows, the movement of planets, the behavior of animals, and changing weather conditions. They learned that by recognizing chi in a landscape they could determine which locations would be safe from danger, provide good growing sources for food, and align harmoniously with the earth. Through the observation of natural forces, they invented the magnetic compass and formed a system of astrological prediction. As a result of all of these observations, the science of feng shui, the art of placement, was born.

Feng shui was used by the ancient Chinese to choose the best places for homes, villages, and palaces. It was also used to determine the correct time and place to construct public works such as bridges. This same science was used to locate graveyards so that the chi of the deceased would continue to support their descendants. Today feng shui is applied in both the East and West to private homes, public buildings, and city centers.

How Feng Shui Saved China

When the colonial powers of the West moved into China at the end of the last century, the feng shui masters were mobilized by the Chinese government to fight the barbarians. The Manchu (or Ch'ing) was China's last imperial dynasty, which was overthrown in 1911. But the middle of the nineteenth century marked the beginning of the end of this dynasty. For two centuries the Manchu rulers had brought a surge of expansion and a flowering of culture. At the time that the American colonies were struggling to achieve their independence, the empire of China had reached the farthest boundaries in its history. Yet, within a generation, the empire had begun to crumble. Drugs began to infiltrate China. British merchants had drugs to sell—opium in particular. The Chinese market was a potentially rich one for the British merchants. However, the Chinese government proved to be uncooperative. The Manchu rulers felt that opium was bad for their people and refused to allow the British to bring it into China. The Manchu rulers wrote a letter to Victoria, "Queen of All the Barbarians," to plead with her and her government to cease their pressure upon the Chinese to accept shipments of opium.

The pressure escalated. The British government would not allow the Chinese to restrict British opium merchants. The government of Queen Victoria declared war on the Chinese and forced them to allow the importation of opium, missionaries, and the British colonization of

*Chinese ports. It was open season in China. Soon the French got a piece
of the action. They, too, got opium privileges and a few Chinese ports.
The Russians followed and then the Germans.*

*There was little the dying Ch'ing dynasty could do to retaliate. They
had to relinquish land to the foreigners. The Manchus called in old and
wise men to select the sites for the foreigners. The old wise men came with
their strange apparatuses and funny-looking compasses. They chose the
sites and the foreigners occupied them.*

*Strange things occurred on these sites selected by the old men.
Illnesses erupted among the foreign occupiers. The population deterior-
ated rapidly. The housing built on the island of Shamien was overrun by
ruinous white ants. The old men had chosen well. They were feng shui
masters instructed by their government to pick the worst sites for the
foreign barbarians. They did.*

—SARVANANDA BLUESTONE, PH.D., FROM
HOW TO READ SIGNS AND OMENS IN EVERYDAY LIFE

You may find it hard to believe that painting your room a particular
color or where you place your bed and stash your gear might influence how
well you do at your next sports event. But throughout Asia it is common
knowledge that the success or failure of a business is dependent upon the
design of the physical space in which it is located. The concept of using
design elements to influence circumstances is also not unfamiliar to the
West. The ancient Greeks used architecture to encourage democratic
interaction, with large, institutional columns leading to open centers.
Different types of cathedrals were built in different periods of European
history to evoke sentiments that range from Gothic fear of the divine to
peaceful reverence. The Egyptian and Mayan pyramids were brilliantly
designed in ways similar to the wisdom of feng shui.

Begin with the Eight Areas of Life

According to feng shui principles, your life can be divided into eight major areas of interest: Knowledge, Family/Health, Wealth, Fame/Reputation, Relationships/Romance, Creativity/Children, Helpful people/Travel, and Career. Some of these areas have dual significance: Family includes Health, because we inherit much of our health from our family; Fame can be interpreted as Reputation; Relationships includes Romance; and Creativity is associated with Children because it is tied to the powerful forces of fertility (in part 3 of this book, we will look more closely at each area and what it includes). As you learn feng shui, you'll develop the skill of identifying what part of any room matches up with each of the eight areas of life. Then you can make choices about what you want in each area in order to have good energy flowing in all aspects of your life.

THE EIGHT AREAS OF LIFE

Knowledge	Relationships/Romance
Family/Health	Creativity/Children
Wealth	Helpful people/Travel
Fame/Reputation	Career

ACTIVITY: THE EIGHT AREAS OF YOUR LIFE

Take a close look at how you feel about each of these eight areas of your life. Rank each area from 1 to 8, number 1 being the area most important to you and number 8 the least important. Think about what your goals are for each area. If you like you can make notes in the space provided below. Write down today's date, so you can revisit your notes and observe how your goals shift and change with time.

Today's Date:_____

Area of Life	Rating (1–8)	Goals
Knowledge		
Family/Health		
Wealth		
Fame/Reputation		
Relationships/Romance		
Creativity/Children		
Helpful people/Travel		
Career		

Don't feel bad if you don't know what your goals are for some of these life areas. That is appropriate: the teen years are the time of life to explore, to try new things, to figure out what you really want for yourself. Feng shui is a great tool to use for this process, so read on!

Which Feng Shui?

Think of how many English teachers you have had in school and how they each taught in a different way, even though they were all teaching English. Imagine, then, how many different schools and styles of feng shui could have developed over 5,000 years! Many different teachers and masters have emerged throughout the ages to develop the art and science of feng shui. The benefit of all of these voices is that the core principles of feng shui have been applied in numerous ways, for countless societies. The less beneficial side is that you, as a new student of feng shui, may find it confusing to wade through all of the different schools. To simplify things, know that there are two major feng shui styles used in the United States. They are the Black Hat style and the Compass style. One big difference between these two styles is the way each determines what part of your room corresponds to what part of your life. Practitioners of the compass style might use a map such as the one below called the *lo p'an*. In Chinese, *lo* means "spiral" and *p'an* means "plate." This compass is configured as a banded plate with a rounded bottom line, like a saucer.

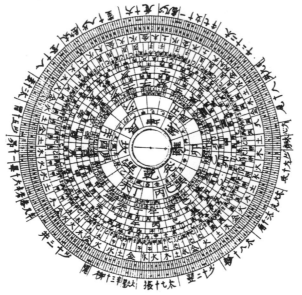

The Lo P'an Compass

Why the term Black Hat? There are different sects of Tibetan Buddhism. Each sect has unique spiritual qualities that make their Buddhist practice slightly different from the others. Monks of some sects are distinguished by the color of their hats: black hats, red hats, yellow hats, and so on. Grand Master Lin Yun Rinpoche, teacher of the style of feng shui presented in this book, is of the Black Hat lineage.

Does it look complicated? It is. A feng shui master of this style would have to spend many, many years in apprenticeship in an Asian country to learn the cultural subtleties that are necessary to properly interpret the lo p'an. In large cities in the United States one can find consultants who practice this classical form of feng shui.

Black Hat style combines observation, intuition, and common sense with the basic principles of feng shui to apply feng shui in cultural contexts outside of China. It has tools that are much easier to use yet still are very powerful and effective. The feng shui style used in this book is the Black Hat style taught by His Holiness, Grand Master Lin Yun Rinpoche, a Chinese master of Tibetan Buddhist lineage. He designed a way to do feng shui by applying a universal diagram called the *ba-gua* (pronounced "bah gwah") to any room or building.

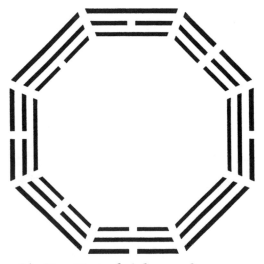

Lin Yun Rinpoche's ba-gua diagram

2

The Way of Chi

We talked a little in chapter 1 about how chi is the invisible energy that moves through all things—the life force. Chi is in constant movement, through our bodies, the earth, and even our rooms. There is chi in your locker and chi in your dresser drawers. It is because of chi that you can lift your arm or inhale and exhale.

If your body doesn't have enough chi, you will find yourself tired or sick. If you have too much chi, you might be restless and unable to concentrate. The goal is to attain a balance of chi, so that you are healthy, vital, and in synch with your environment. In acupuncture, the Chinese medical practice based on the same principles as feng shui, doctors locate areas in the body where chi is blocked. They apply a remedy to release chi and restore balance to the body. Or they may notice an area where chi is escaping from the body and use a remedy to seal the leak.

Similarly, when chi is in harmony and balance in our living spaces, we can live in a state of peace. This is the purpose of feng shui. Some places have naturally balanced chi, such as where mountain peaks join a watery plain. In those places, the chi is smooth, harmonious, and inspires meditation. Ancient feng shui masters knew how to choose those spots as sacred sites for temples or power places for government buildings. When a building is located where the chi is in natural harmony, it is considered particularly lucky.

Known in Sanskrit as *prana,* and in English as *ether,* chi is also translated as *ki* or *qi.* Chi is the vital energy in our body and every living thing.

The Way Chi Moves

Since your feng shui practice will be based on arranging objects to create balanced chi, it's useful for us to know a little about how chi works. Chi moves like the wind through open spaces. Just as water in a river is directed by its banks and diverted by rocks or trees that have fallen in, chi is also directed and diverted by objects. We can observe the natural tendencies of chi by looking at rings in a tree stump, ripples in a pond, and sand patterns in wind-blown dunes. When left uninterrupted by interfering objects, chi travels in a curve (there are few straight lines in nature). When chi can be charted and mapped, the resulting lines are called "dragon lines." Dragon lines depict hidden meridians, the curving grid lines of energy that travel across and below the earth's surface. (These same meridians run through our body and are the basis of Chinese acupuncture.) Special meridian points form sacred spaces on earth, similar to pressure points within the human body. The Chinese used these dragon lines to direct them to lucky building sites. The most famous building on a dragon line is the Great Wall of China. You will notice that the Great Wall of China is not built on a straight line, but instead flows with the curve of chi in the landscape.

But the Great Wall of China also provides an example of how ignoring the principles of chi can result in disaster. Though the builders of the Great Wall respected the curving motion of chi, the original builders from the Ch'in dynasty were unfortunately forced to build across the dragon lines at a few points, rather than tracing the dragon lines or building alongside of them. Crossing dragon lines results in blocked chi, which is considered very unlucky in feng shui. The Ch'in dynasty only lasted fifteen years. Many credit the quick demise of this dynasty to the unfortunate crossing of dragon lines during the construction of the Great Wall.

The Great Wall of China is an example of a construction built on a dragon line.

When Chi Goes Out of Balance

Sha chi:
Chi that is harmful and toxic.

Chi naturally travels in circles and curves. When it is forced to move in a straight line, it travels like a projectile, as if it were a bullet or an arrow. This can cause harm to whatever is on the receiving end. When chi is forced to move in this manner, it creates negative or potentially harmful energy that is called *sha chi*. Sha chi carries energy that is unfavorable to one's own health and can have an adverse effect on other people.

Geologically speaking, sha chi is produced by fault lines and fissures in the earth. Glare from the sun is also a source of sha chi. Sha chi can enter buildings through the cracks in walls and broken windows. It accumulates in empty or dirty corners and sharp angles, and travels at fast speeds when forced to follow a straight line. Overcrowded places generate sha chi, which is increased by glaring lights, loud noises, and bad smells. In short, sha chi is toxic chi. Modern urban design, with its emphasis on the linear, is a major generator of sha chi.

Shiny Sha

Objects that are too shiny can create sha chi. Shiny objects will compete with everything around them for energy, depleting your room or house of vital chi. Examples of negative shine can be light reflecting off water or parked cars. When a highly reflective surface is combined with a pointed shape the result can be doubly disastrous because sha chi is both collected and focused into sharp arrows, like a laser beam.

Yin + Yang = Tao

Before Heaven and Earth were separate there was only the indefinable ONE. This One was divided and yin and yang came into existence. That which received yang chi rose up bright and clear and became Heaven; that which received yin chi sank down heavy and obscure and became Earth; and that which received both yin chi and yang chi in right proportions became man.
—THE *EXPERIENCE OF THE GOLDEN FLOWER*, TAOIST TEXT

Thirty spokes join together in a single
wheel,
but it is the center hole
that makes the wagon move
We shape a lump of clay into a vessel,
but it is the emptiness inside the vessel
that makes it useful
We hammer doors and windows of wood
for a house,
but it is the empty inner space
that makes room livable
We build with the tangible,
but the intangible is what we use.
—LAO-TZU, FROM THE *TAO TE CHING*

According to the ancient masters, chi has two primary characteristics: there is yin chi and yang chi. Yin chi is energy that is feminine, receptive, dark, and representative of the mysterious forces of shadow and the subconscious. Yang chi is masculine, creative, light, and representative of that which is visible in daytime or evident on the surface. Together, they compose the Tao, the whole of the universe.

The Taoist philosopher Lao-tzu (born 640 B.C.) was the author of the *Tao Te Ching*, also known as the Way of Virtue. In this book, Taoist wisdom is condensed into 81 short chapters of verse. Lao-tzu understood that we can live in perfect grace, harmony, and truth by accepting change in life, just as the natural world accepts change in nature. According to the Taoists, all energy is interconnected. There is no concept of sin, and evil is not condemned. Lao-tzu explained the relationship between yin and yang:

> When some things are deemed beautiful
> other things become ugly.
> When things are deemed good,

What is Tao?

There was something formless and perfect

before the universe was born.

It is serene. Empty.

Solitary. Unchanging.

Infinite. Eternally present.

It is the mother of the universe.

For lack of a better name, I call it the Tao.

It flows through all things,

inside and outside, and returns

to the origin of all things.

The Tao is great.

The universe is great.

Earth is great.

Each human is great.

These are the four great powers.

A human follows the earth.

Earth follows the universe.

The universe follows the Tao.

The Tao follows only itself.

— LAO-TZU, FROM *TAO TE CHING*

Other things become bad.

Existence and nonexistence create each other.

Difficulty and easy produce each other.

Long and short are fashioned from each other.

High and low contrast each other.

Before and behind follow each other.

The interaction between yin chi and yang chi is constant and creates change in our universe. Therefore, if we wish to create change in our lives, the first place to start is in exploring the relationship between our yin chi and yang chi. In the symbol of the Tao, we can see how these two energies interact within the universe.

Yin and Yang

We all have an intuitive capacity to feel chi. If you were to stand near a waterfall in the mountains with its powerful rush, you would experience the exhilaration of the positive yang chi coming from the speed of the water. But if you were to sit near a soft fountain in a quiet park, you would experience the soothing relaxation of yin chi. A bustling coffee shop with bright lights and the sound of espresso machines is bursting with yang energy, whereas a quiet flower shop is more likely to invoke gentle yin energy.

The word *yang* is usually associated with masculinity and *yin* with femininity, but men and women both possess yin and yang qualities.

In the yin-yang symbol on page 24, the black area represents yin and the white area is yang. There is a black dot in the large white shape and a white dot in the large black shape—yang within yin and yin within yang. Neither yin nor yang are absolute; they always possess a portion of their opposite. This is the sacred dance of yin and yang.

YIN	YANG
Earth	Heaven
Valley	Mountain
Cyclic	Linear
Black	White
Dark	Light
Female	Male
Moon	Sun
Water	Fire
Wet	Dry
Cold	Hot
Slow	Fast
Passive	Active
Receptive	Assertive
Round	Angular
Smooth	Rough

YIN ACTIVITIES	YANG ACTIVITIES
Reading	Running
Gardening	Extreme sports
Listening to music	Dancing

YIN-YANG QUIZ FOR YOUR ROOM

You can use the "tuning in" skills you developed with the exercise on pages 9–11 to help you intuit the balance (or lack thereof) between yin and yang in any space. Fill out the following quiz to observe how much yin and how much yang is in your room.

Directions:

In a few words, answer the six questions below. Observe whether your answers reflect yin or yang energy by reading the description below each question. Circle either "yin" or "yang" in the column at the far right to indicate your observation.

1. What do you feel when you enter your room?_____

_____

_____

Energetic, anxious, and rushed feelings are yang. Feelings of relaxation, boredom, and sleepiness are yin.   Yin/Yang

2. What sounds do you hear?_____

_____

_____

Rock, rap, or heavy metal are yang, as are footsteps in fast motion, fast speed trains, and honking horns. Gentle babbling brooks, soft music, and silence are all yin.   Yin/Yang

3. What do you smell?_____

_____

_____

Strong, pungent cooking smells, body odors, or crisp citrus-based air fresheners are yang. Lavender candles, dampness, or the scent of moist soil are yin.   Yin/Yang

4. What is the climate like?_____

_____

_____

Hot is yang and cold is yin.   Yin/Yang

5. What colors dominate your room?_____

_____

_____

Bright and colorful surroundings are yang, while muted light and soft
colors are yin.   Yin/Yang

6. When you touch the items around you, are they hard and yang or
   soft and yin? _____

_____

_____

                                                                Yin/Yang

Now count your answers:

Total Yin: _____   Total Yang:_____

Do you have more yin than yang, more yang than yin, or are they
balanced? Repeat this exercise in your room at different times of day,
on different days of the week. You will notice that the energy of your
room may shift dramatically based on changes in lighting—strong
midday sun as opposed to nighttime darkness, for example—and
changes in human behavior, such as sound pollution from commuter
traffic during the week that lessens on the weekends. As you practice
tuning in to the sights and sensations around you, the difference
between yin and yang will become increasingly clear to you. You can
practice this exercise in any space, at any time.

Because the bedroom is where we sleep, rest, and regenerate our bodies, the bedroom should be yin. Ideally, one should avoid doing activities such as work, creative projects, eating, exercise, and watching TV in the bedroom. This creates a challenge for teens who use their bedroom as command central for their life. So how do you reconcile these energy forces and use them to your advantage? In chapter 4 you can read about bedroom basics and how you can incorporate yang energy into certain areas of your room without disturbing your sleep. In the upcoming chapters, you're going to begin moving things around in your room. Keep the yin-yang balance in mind. The goal is to have a bedroom that is predominantly yin but that possesses enough yang to create balance. If, after rearranging your room, you still feel like your room is too yang or too yin, consult the feng shui cures offered in chapter 14.

Primal Energies

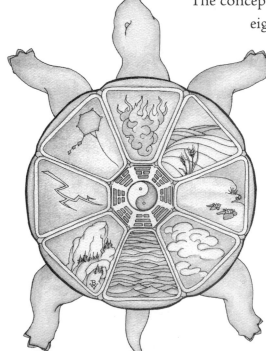

The concepts that formulate feng shui are based on eight *trigrams*—symbols comprised of three stacked lines. The ancient Chinese King Fu Shi is said to have created these trigrams during his rule, 3,000 years ago. The legend goes that one day, as Fu Shi sat meditating by the Yellow River, he watched a tortoise emerge from the water. During this meditation, Fu Shi observed the markings on the tortoise shell and saw how the primal energies of the universe could be depicted by the eight

Fu Shi saw the primal energies of the universe on the back of a tortoise shell.

trigrams. These trigrams represent phenomena in the physical world: mountain, thunder, wind, fire, earth, lake, heaven, and water. These eight trigrams are born from yin energy (represented by a broken line) and yang energy (represented by a solid line), as shown in the diagram below.

Remember the eight areas of your life you rated for yourself in chapter 1? Well, each gua of the eight trigrams corresponds to one of those eight areas. And in feng shui, each trigram/area of your life corresponds to one area of your room.

Trigrams: Chinese symbols comprised of three stacked lines. The lines are either yin (represented by a broken line) or yang (represented by a solid line). Eight trigrams represent all phenomena of the physical world: mountain, thunder, wind, fire, earth, lake, heaven, and water.

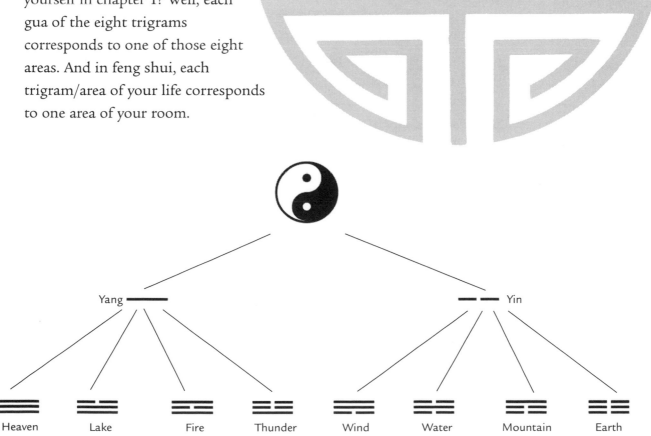

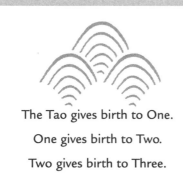

The Tao gives birth to One.

One gives birth to Two.

Two gives birth to Three.

Three gives birth to ten thousand things.

—LAO-TZU IN THE *TAO TE CHING*

Mountain = Knowledge

Like a hermit meditating in a mountain cave, we can call on the energy of Mountain to assist us with development of knowledge. Mountain's trigram is composed of two broken yin lines below a solid yang line. Under the solid top is a space, indicating a cave inside a mountain. Mountain is for the completion of all things. Mountains are for bringing all things to conclusion and gain. Nothing is more perfect than Mountain. Huge, immobile Mountain presents meditation, movement halted, and resting of the body, mind, and spirit. You can imagine the intimacy within a cave from the bottom two yin lines, yet a sense of protection and covering from the top solid line.

Thunder = Family/Health

The strength and power of Thunder is like the voice of ancestors and parents, teachers, and other authority figures. Health is linked to family because many illnesses are inherited. Thunder hits solidly and rises to disperse. Thunder represents dynamic movement, activity, vitality, development, and growth. Thunder is for agitating all things. Nothing is swifter than Thunder. You can imagine the force of Thunder by studying its three lines. The bottom yang line indicates how strong Thunder is when it hits. But as it rises, it opens to join the air and becomes yin.

Wind = Wealth

Good fortune, wealth, and prosperity can come your way easily as if carried on the wind. This trigram also represents blessings and opportunities, not just money. Wind is for stirring all things. Nothing is more effective than Wind. Success can be achieved through yielding to superior forces and new opportunities. Wind represents pliability, penetration, influence from others, and flexibility. Imagine the bottom line as a safe little crawl space where the wind can enter, as if it is a small crevice protected by solid lines.

Fire = Fame/Reputation

Just as a fire glows brightly, so can your reputation. Fire indicates your dynamic chi in the world. The greater your fire, the greater your fame. Fire is for drying up all things. Nothing is more drying than Fire. Knowledge and wisdom shine as a bright flame to ensure and maintain good fortune. Fire represents expansion, ideas, illumination, clarity, brilliance, and beauty. This trigram represents a flame, which is solid on the top and bottom, yet open in the middle.

Earth = Relationships/Romance

The earth is open to receive sun, rain, and seeds. We too must be open to receive in order to create loving relationships. Earth is the most yin of all the trigrams. Earth is the complement to Heaven. Earth is for nurturing all things. Earth represents the great female principle by which all things are nurtured, the femininity of Mother Earth, the receptive and yielding principle. All three lines are broken, indicating that this trigram is completely yin.

Lake = Creativity/Children

A peaceful lake is childlike, safe, and inspirational—the perfect state for creativity to flourish. Lake is open and receptive on the surface, yet contains mass below. Lake is for satisfying all things and nothing is more gratifying than Lake. Lake encourages development of virtues. Lake represents joy, happiness, pleasure, contentment, and possible excess. One way to imagine the peace of a lake is to visualize a lily or lotus floating on the water. There is gentle movement on the surface, yet the water is solid and deep.

Heaven = Helpful People/Travel

Those who help you are like guardians or angels sent from Heaven. Just as the stars of the night sky guide sailors to their destination, so the energies of Heaven guide the destiny of the traveler. Heaven represents the celestial forces generating all things. It is the creative source, perfection, strength, vitality, originality, and power. Heaven is strong and undivided. It is most yang, the great male principle. This symbol shows that all things are properly ordered: the sun shines, rain falls, and people prosper. You can imagine the strength and power of the Heaven chi by observing its symbol of three solid lines. The trigram is completely yang.

Water = Career

Your work, career, or calling is like the river of life as you follow its winding path. Water may seem clear and uniform, but it has a solid mass in the center. A wave will crash when the surface of the water moves at a faster rate than the solid central mass. Water is for moistening all things; nothing is more humid than water. Water represents mystery, profound meaning, and possible danger. You can imagine Water moving because its top and bottom lines are yin. Yet the core is very strong, as indicated by the solid yang line in the center.

The Ba-gua

After discerning the eight primal energies behind all phenomenon of the physical universe, Fu Shi placed the trigrams in the octagon shape of the tortoise shell to show how the universe is ordered. This became known as the *ba-gua,* or the eight trigrams. In Chinese, *Ba* means "eight" and *gua* means "trigram."

According to feng shui principles, everywhere we go, at any given time, we are surrounded by the eight guas, the eight areas of life. When they are out of balance, we feel scattered, sick, or confused. But when the eight areas of life are all working in synch rather against each other, they act as an invisible force field to protect us and help us reach our goals. It is the aim of feng shui masters to re-create the natural order—represented by the ba-gua—in all settings. You don't have to be a feng shui master, however, to apply simple practices to improve the balance and synchronicity in your living environment and your life. All it takes is a little practice working with chi and a good road map.

Ba-gua: The term used for the map that shows how the universe is ordered. *Ba* is the Chinese word for "eight." *Gua* is the Chinese word for "trigram," a symbol comprised of three stacked lines.

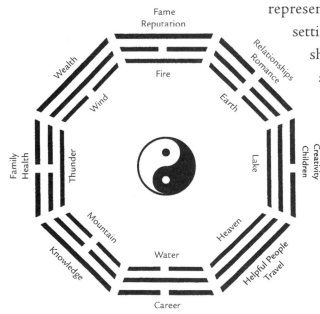

The eight areas of life correspond to the trigrams of the ba-gua.

Using the Ba-gua Map

Mouth of Chi: The place from which the most chi enters a space, usually the front door or an entranceway.

You can find the eight areas in your room by first determining where chi, life energy, enters the room. How do you know where the chi is entering your room? Simple. Wherever the main door is, the one you most frequently use to enter the space from the outside, is called the "Mouth of Chi" (we'll be discussing how to work with the mouth of chi further in chapter 3).

As you can see from the diagram below, the mouth of chi will be in one of three places: the middle of a wall, the right hand side of a wall, or the left hand side of a wall.

Once you have identified the mouth of chi, you can determine where all eight areas of your life reside in your space:

Knowledge is in the near left corner when you enter

Family/Health is in the middle left wall when you enter

Wealth is in the far left corner

Fame/Reputation is in the farthest point from where you enter, the center of the back wall

Relationships/Romance is in the far right corner

Creativity/Children is the middle of the right wall when you enter

Helpful people/Travel is the near right corner when you enter

Career is the middle wall closest to where you enter

In the center of the space is the tao.

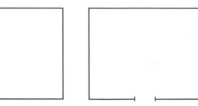

The mouth of chi will be in one of these three locations.

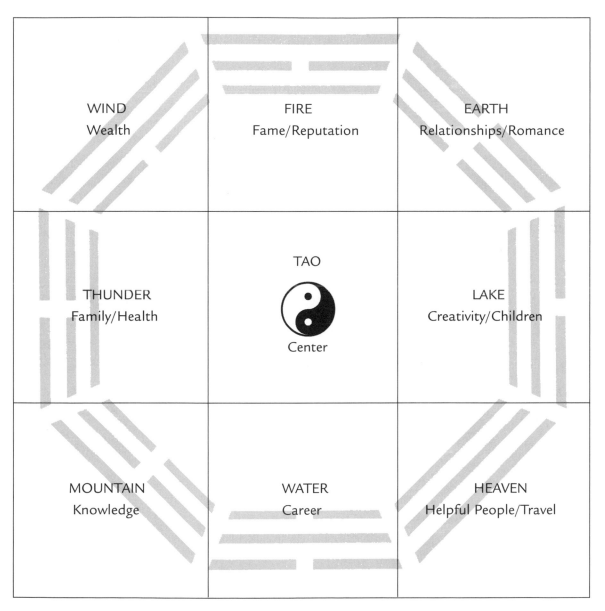

WIND Wealth	FIRE Fame/Reputation	EARTH Relationships/Romance
THUNDER Family/Health	TAO Center	LAKE Creativity/Children
MOUNTAIN Knowledge	WATER Career	HEAVEN Helpful People/Travel

The ba-gua map is applied to the room by orienting guas to the mouth of chi.
Place the ba-gua so that Mountain, Water, and Heaven guas share
a wall with the mouth of chi (the door to your room).

Once you learn to apply the ba-gua map to your room, you can apply it anywhere: the rooms of friends, the other rooms of your house, and the house as a whole (see chapter 17 for more details on applying feng shui to the whole house).

Help! My Room Shape Is Weird!

Not all buildings are designed in a perfect square or rectangle. When placing the ba-gua map over your room, you might find the room has a projection or extra space such as a porch or patio. This is a natural enhancement that will positively increase the power of that area, so you are lucky it's there. Likewise, a room that is missing a section in a particular gua means you will need to compensate for that area using some of the tricks and "cures" we will discuss in chapter 14.

Don't panic if your room does not exactly fit the ba-gua. Throughout your feng shui practice you are bound to find some areas in which the specifics of your situation will not be ideal. Slanted ceilings, a room being too narrow and long, exposed beams, and many other details can all create a chi imbalance or sha chi. For now, don't worry too much about your room being less-than-perfect. Map out the eight areas of your room, and simply make note of any questions that come up.

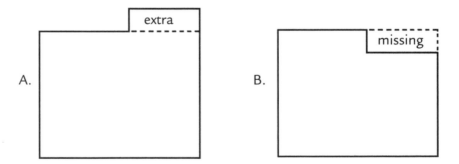

You might find that your room has extra space or is missing space where a gua should be. In example A, there is an extra space in the Relationships/Romance gua. In example B, the Relationships/Romance gua is missing space.

Where Are Your Shoes?

He was a Zen Master. And it was not easy being a Zen Master, for many would-be disciples came from all parts of Japan to seek his guidance. But he lived in a modest cottage in the mountains and let the aspiring disciples come as they would.

One day a young man arrived at the Master's cottage. This was a young man who was quite serious about his spiritual path. This acolyte had studied much, meditated much, and felt that he was quite ready to become the right-hand disciple of any Master.

It had been raining when the young man arrived at the Master's house. The Master was seated on a pillow in a small room. The young man carefully removed his shoes and placed his umbrella outside the door.

The young man entered the room and bowed to the Master. "I would like to become your disciple. I would like to become enlightened as you are, Master," the young man said.

"I have studied much and feel that I am on the path to realization," said the young man, growing a bit uncomfortable at the Master's silence.

The Master smiled with his eyes half-closed and nodded.

"Don't you feel that I could become an awakened one?" asked the youth, becoming exasperated at the Master's reticence.

The Master opened his eyes. The young man now felt hopeful. The Master would accept him.

"Do you know on which side of the door you placed your umbrella and on which side you placed your shoes?" asked the Master quietly.

"N-n-n-no," stuttered the young man, disconcerted. "Why?"

"Because," answered the Master slowly, "what you seek is awareness. And how can you be aware if you do not even know where you have put your shoes and umbrella?"

—SARVANANDA BLUESTONE PH.D., FROM *HOW TO READ SIGNS AND OMENS IN EVERYDAY LIFE*

ACTIVITY: MAPPING THE AREAS OF LIFE IN YOUR ROOM

Using the grid on the next page and overlapping the ba-gua map, make a drawing of the areas of your room and their contents.

- First draw the shape of your room over the grid, orienting your drawing so that the primary entrance to your room is at the bottom of the page, matched up with the Knowledge–Career–Helpful people section of the ba-gua. Note the shape of your room: is it square, rectangular, or irregular?

- Mark the mouth of chi with two vertical lines: ▮ ▮

- Identify any windows with an extra-thick line along the wall where the window appears: ▬▬▬▬

- Note any closets or built-in structures (such as columns or built-in furniture) with a dotted line: ▬ ▬ ▬ ▬

- In pencil, mark where the major pieces of furniture are: bed, dressers, additional doors, bookshelves, desks, TV, computer, exercise equipment, and so forth.

This will be your guide for applying the helpful wisdom of feng shui to your life! Take a moment to see what you have in each area of your life.

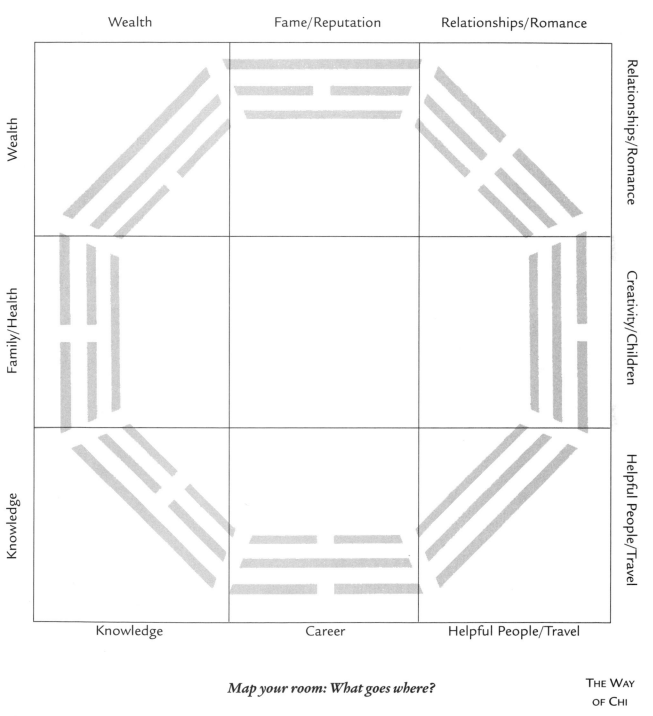

Wealth   Fame/Reputation   Relationships/Romance

Wealth

Family/Health

Knowledge

Relationships/Romance

Creativity/Children

Helpful People/Travel

Knowledge   Career   Helpful People/Travel

Map your room: What goes where?

Part Two

Getting Started

ow that you know which area of your room corresponds to which area of your life, the art and fun of feng shui can really begin. The next few chapters will show you how to prepare your room for a feng shui makeover. You'll learn about the three basics around which a feng shui practice can best be accomplished. You'll also find simple tips on bedroom energy and proper placement for larger items in order to maximize the positive chi in each of the eight guas.

3

The Three Basics

f there is anything I wish for you to take from this entire book, it is what
I consider to be the three basics of feng shui. These are the three most
powerful actions you can take to immediately improve your room and
your life:

1. **Remove clutter.** Open spaces allow chi to flow freely and fluidly
    throughout the room. Clutter creates chaotic chi. And new energy
    cannot enter a space that is full of unconscious clutter and mess.

2. **Keep an open mouth of chi.** This means making sure that the
    doorway or entrance where chi enters a space is free of obstacles so
    that chi can move in and out freely.

3. **Place your objects in the appropriate gua.** This means determining
    which part of your room corresponds to which of the eight life areas
    and then placing appropriate objects in that gua in order to create
    balance and support your goals.

Sounds pretty simple, right? Except that in all the years of my practice
as a feng shui consultant the three most common feng shui no-nos that I
see in practically every household are, you guessed it: clutter, blocked
mouth of chi, and poor object placement.

The different styles of feng shui that we discussed in chapter 2 all have different ways of achieving these three basics, but in concept they are present in every single feng shui practice. If you can understand these three basics, you can apply feng shui anytime, anywhere.

Clutter = Chaos

Sometimes it seems as if our lifestyle is built on the consumption and possession of stuff. In ads and billboards, we're told to buy the latest computer game or designer pair of sneakers in order to succeed and live out our dreams. So we go out and buy those sneakers or that computer game and, next thing you know, there's another shoe or computer game on the market that we believe we absolutely "must" have. But where does the old stuff go, once we're on to newer and better things? Usually into the land of "I might wear that again if I'm in the mood" or "I'll read that someday," in other words, clutter! These lands of forgotten or spent energies spread out from our closets and onto floors and desk space until, suddenly, they've taken over. Like used plastic shopping bags stuck on the branches of a riverbank tree, our clutter poisons our view and enjoyment of the objects that we *do* need and want and use.

Out with the Old, In with the New!

Just as an artist begins a painting with a clean, freshly prepared canvas, in order to successfully create your "new" room—and life—it needs to be clear of clutter. Clutter blocks both mental and physical chi, not to mention that you will find it hard to move your bed and other things around if you can't even see the floor! When you clear out all the sha energy in your physical and emotional space, you can create room for new, positive chi.

Whether we want to move on from old relationships, old clothes, or old ways of being, we all benefit from the change of energy that comes when we do an "out with the old, in with the new" kind of purge. Here's a secret to keep in mind: you don't have to get rid of everything to get rid of toxic chi; you just need to get rid of clutter. So, what is clutter? Clutter usually consists of three things:

1. Items that are not stored in their proper place so that you are either constantly stumbling over them or can never find them when you want them.

2. Items that you no longer need or use but are somehow managing to take up your storage or surface space.

3. Items that you don't even like but were given as gifts so you feel obligated to keep them.

How do we get rid of clutter? It may sound like a silly question, but many people actually don't know how to organize their possessions. If your room is really messy, the thought of trying to clean it up can be overwhelming. The trick is to take it step-by-step. First go through your mess and figure out what stuff belongs in the following categories:

1. **Essential.** Better not to lose track of this stuff, which consists of current schoolwork, textbooks, gear from a sport, or any other item that is a core part of your day.

2. **Favorites.** These are items that you truly like and enjoy, such as momentos and photos of friends. Valuable and fragile items such as jewelry, art pieces, and musical instruments also fit into this category.

3. **Other people's stuff.** This is anything borrowed from friends or placed in your room by a sibling or other household member. This category can also include library books or video rentals that are overdue and ready to be returned. Sometimes this category will also include items of clothing or used books that you plan to give away, donate, or trade.

4. **Annoying.** Junk mail, laundry, and old magazines are examples of life's little annoyances that frequently end up in our spaces.

5. **Downright gross.** Dirty dishes, leftover pizza, or super-stinky socks— gross is gross. You should be able to identify it when you see it.

Now jump to action and claim your power to change your life:

❷ **Get rid of the gross**—dump it in the garbage, soak it in the sink, or disinfect it with an antibacterial household product.

❷ **Sort through the annoying** with a strong sense of clarity. Don't need it? Get rid of it. Clip and file any articles from old magazines and recycle the magazine (you can reduce magazine clutter by recycling the old magazine as soon as the new one arrives). Store annoying things out of sight—in filing cabinets, closets, boxes, or drawers.

❷ **Put other people's stuff in a box** outside of your room and return the stuff as soon as possible.

❷ **Make a plan for where you want your favorites to go.** Loose pictures should go in photo albums, frames, or storage boxes. If you don't have a special place for jewelry make or purchase a jewelry box. Favorite possessions are usually items that you want on display, so plan on offering a little shelf space to them. Consider placing favorites in areas where young siblings or animals can't get to them and damage them.

❷ **Make sure that your essentials are easy to access.** Store them in the same place every day so that you always know where to find them.

Now revisit your categories and check off each item as it is accomplished:

☐ Gross is gone.

☐ Annoying is minimized and put out of sight.

☐ Other people's stuff is returned.

☐ Favorites are given a place of honor.

☐ Essentials are located where they are easy to access.

What's left? **CLUTTER.**

Clear that clutter off desks, dressers, bookshelves, bed, and everywhere else in your room. Put it in a big pile. Examine all of the items making up this clutter pile. Which of these have you outgrown? What things are not really important to you and are just taking up space? Recycle, throw out, or place in a bag to give away. Then get the stuff out of your room. Place the things you want to keep on shelves, in drawers, or in boxes. Keep going until the pile is gone.

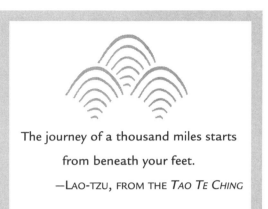

The journey of a thousand miles starts from beneath your feet.

—LAO-TZU, FROM THE *TAO TE CHING*

If a few things have become an important part of your past, spend a few hours making a photo album or portfolio of your favorite pictures, notes, and creative projects of your younger years or decorate a shoe box as a treasure box to store your precious things. Place it in the attic, basement, or closet to be reopened years later to remember the magic of your past.

Vintage Clothing

Used clothes and antiques purchased from thrift stores or yard sales retain the chi of the previous owners. This is why you might find certain used objects just seem to feel good and others do not. Clothing and furniture that have known previous owners may retain the love and luck that person experienced with those items, or the items may just as easily retain a sense of tragedy or bad luck. Use your intuition to sense whether items have positive energy. Is that antique party hat you picked up at the funky used clothing store a little creepy? Listen to your initial reactions. If something about an item feels off to you, don't use it.

The good news is that most hand-me-downs or vintage pieces don't always retain strong chi and will soon possess your own chi after a good wash and a few wears. Many world traditions use energy-cleansing rituals on a regular basis. In the United States, the most common form of energy cleansing is with water: laundry, showers, and baptisms. In some Jewish traditions previously owned plates and silverware can be cleansed and made kosher through a ritual dip in boiling water. Many Native American cultures in North America will purify the energy in a space by passing sage smoke through a room. Contemporary pagans use candles and rituals to cleanse energy. You can consult any of these traditions for energy-clearing rituals, or create your own.

Open the Mouth of Chi

The entrance is the most important part of a room because the mouth of chi determines the orientation of guas in a room. The mouth of chi must not be blocked or cluttered or else chi cannot enter or exit your room.

The steps to unblock the mouth of chi are:

☯ Move any furniture that prevents a door from swinging open completely. Ideally, one should be able to swing a door 180° before hitting a wall. If a wall is preventing the door from swinging fully open, it is even more important that nothing come between that wall and the door.

☯ Make sure the door is fully functional. Don't live for years with squeaky or slightly-out-of-line doors. Take the extra minute or two to fix it. Vegetable oil from the kitchen applied to door hinges will get rid of squeaks; a few minutes with a screwdriver will fix your loose door handle and hinges. Feng shui is about awareness of your environment. Once a door creak is silenced, you'll realize that you no longer have to live with sha sounds.

◑ Avoid placing any furniture in such a way that it obstructs the walking path of someone entering the room. Even if your oiled door silently swings fully open, if someone trips over a couch or a bed within three steps of entering your room, you've managed to block the mouth of chi.

Be sure to clear clutter away from the mouth of chi so that chi freely enters the room. A nice touch is to add a door chime to your entranceway. Have you ever walked into a store and heard the small tinkle of a door chime or bell? A few dangling chimes or even a small bell at the entrance of a room serves to disperse sha chi. It is as if anytime someone enters your room, they are sprinkled with magic fairy dust. Door chimes pleasantly disperse chi and can inform you whenever someone enters or leaves your space so that you are not caught off guard.

Object Placement

By now you've got the message that sections of your room correspond to the eight areas of life and that where you place things in your room matters. The goal of this book is to help you create balance and harmony by placing your items in their best life area, for example, placing books in the knowledge gua.

The next chapter offers some object placement ideas specifically for the large pieces of furniture in your bedroom. You'll also learn about colors and other bedroom features to take into account as you transform your room. Part 3 will then help you refine your personal goals for each of your eight life areas and what is best to place in each gua. Once you memorize the ba-gua map and carry it in your heart, you will understand object placement. For now, let's start with the big stuff.

A Poor Choice of Object Placement

A perfect example of poor object placement is where one couple I worked with in San Francisco kept their cooking knives. Jodi and Mitch were lovely people and appeared to be highly compatible as a couple, showing lots of affection for one another and generally treating each other with a lot of respect. As we walked around the apartment and they discussed with me some of their decorating ideas, it was clear that they enjoyed brainstorming on future plans together. As soon as we entered the kitchen, however, their tone toward each other changed. Mitch began to mock the design tastes of Jodi and Jodi angrily snapped back at him. They both paused for a moment and looked at me sheepishly. One look at their kitchen and I understood exactly what their problem was. Directly above the counter in the Relationships/Romance gua of the kitchen hung a metallic strip, against which were dangling several sharp kitchen knives! Knives might be useful for warriors, but they're certainly not a symbol of romance. I pointed this out to them and they laughed. "We always argue in the kitchen," Mitch confirmed. They quickly purchased a simple wooden knife holder and placed it in an available drawer in their Creativity gua, where it would stay out of trouble. Months later Jodi reported back to me with two thumbs up, saying that their bickering had stopped and she finds the kitchen a much more soothing and relaxed space.

Rearrange Your Room: Change Your Life

n this chapter you'll begin to design your room. The following pages offer some basic guidelines for large furniture placement and color. Once you've absorbed that information you can use the exercise and grid on pages 68 and 69 to create a blueprint for your own room.

Bedroom Energy

The primary function of the bedroom is to provide a restful place for good sleep so the decisions you make about decoration or object placement in your bedroom should support this room's primary function: sleep and rest.

But for teens, your bedroom is also the hub of your independent world: the space in which you work, create, relax, communicate with friends through phone and e-mail, listen to music, and play with fashion. Your bedroom is often the one place where you can experience the most privacy and freedom to be yourself: two resources that are particularly valuable during teen years of exploration and discovery. By applying the ba-gua map to your room, you are on your way to creating change in your life that will bring rewards.

Where Does the Big Stuff Go?

Every item and piece of furniture that you place in your room will impact how you move, what you do, and even what you think about. Look back at the Eight Areas of Your Life chart you created at the end of chapter 1 as you think about the hints given below. By the end of this book, you will know exactly what goes where by using the ba-gua map. But first, move the big pieces of furniture.

Commanding position: The position farthest away from the front door of a room and where the mouth of chi can be easily seen.

The Bed Takes the Commanding Position

Where you put your bed is very important. Your bed is the focal point for chi because you will spend more time there than in any other spot in your room. Approximately one-third of your life is spent in bed. So you want your bed to be in what is known as the *commanding position*. This is the position farthest away from the front door of a room and where the mouth of chi can be seen easily. You want to be able to see your door while lying on the bed.

When an object is placed deep into the room it enhances its strength in that room, giving it greater density and power. The deeper you are nestled into your room, the more control you will have over your environment.

Generals and leaders have been using the commanding position as a means of defending themselves against attackers—always able to see who (or what) is entering their space in order to prepare for potential attacks.

When your bed, or any other piece of furniture, is in the commanding position you are asserting that no one can creep up on you and no activities can go on behind your back. The commanding position is not in direct line with the mouth of chi. Instead it is diagonal—allowing objects and people placed there to sense oncoming energies without getting directly hit by them. If you are in direct line with the mouth of chi, energy will rush at you every time the door is opened or someone enters. You will not have an opportunity to deflect the energy as you would if you were farther away to the side. If the bed is in direct line with the mouth of chi it can result in restlessness and agitation when attempting to sleep. This position—of the bed in direct line with the mouth of chi and with the feet pointed toward the door—is associated with death and is called the *coffin position.*

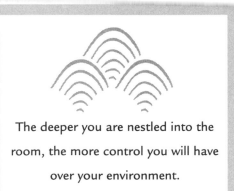

The deeper you are nestled into the room, the more control you will have over your environment.

Avoid sleeping under exposed beams or ceiling fans because these will send poison arrows your way while you sleep. Because you want to be as deep into the room as possible, it is best to avoid placing the bed in one of

Bed Placement Do's and Don'ts

Do's

- *Do* choose the commanding position so that the bed is farthest away from the mouth of chi and so that you can clearly see the mouth of chi when lying on the bed.

- *Do* keep space on both sides of the bed.

Don'ts

- *Don't* sleep under poison arrows such as those caused by ceiling fans or exposed beams.

- *Don't* place the bed in coffin position directly in line with the mouth of chi.

Poison Arrows

Poison arrows are straight lines, sharp angles, or focal points that create sha chi and direct it toward a specific location. A poison arrow of chi is like having a finger pointed at you. It's intimidating. Any sharp object pointing toward the house, your room, or you is a poison arrow. These can be both natural and man-made objects, such as tree branches, sharp rocks, electrical transformers on power lines, fences, construction cranes, and even billboards. An example of a secret arrow in practice is the Bank of China that was built in Hong Kong in 1987. Its sharp angles send sha chi racing directly toward the governor's mansion that neighbors it. Because the governor's personal chi has a major effect on local politics, the negative aspect of the Bank of China influenced the whole of Hong Kong. When the British returned Hong Kong to Chinese control in 1999, the governor's position became obsolete altogether and the heart of the government was moved. Some say this is the direct result of the negative feng shui.

the guas near the door—Helpful people/Travel, Career, or Knowledge. Your bed should also be off the floor. This lifts the chi to a more balanced height.

The headboard of your bed should always be against a wall. This creates a sense of security and stability. It is ideal to have even space on both sides of the bed to create a sense of balance. This is particularly important if two people are sharing a bed, as the one with more space to their side will gain a dominant role in the relationship. (If you share your room with someone, refer to page 90 for advice on bed locations.)

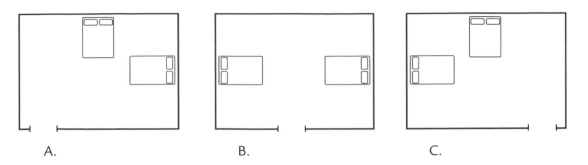

A.   B.   C.

Where to place your bed will depend on the location of the mouth of chi. The commanding position will be the position farthest away from the mouth of chi and where you can see the mouth of chi clearly. In example A, the mouth of chi is in the Knowledge gua and the commanding position can be found in both the Fame/Reputation gua and the Creativity gua. In example B, the mouth of chi is in the Career gua and the commanding position can be in either the Family/Health gua or the Creativity gua. In example C, the mouth of chi is in the Helpful people/Travel gua. The commanding position can be found in either the Fame/Reputation gua or the Family/Health gua.

As you can see in the diagram above, you may have more than one choice for placing your bed in the commanding position. As a living being, you carry vital chi into any space you enter, so the gua you choose for bed placement will naturally receive an energy boost from your sleeping presence. If you have more than one area in your room that would serve as commanding position for the bed, decide which of those areas of your life you want to bring the most energy to right now.

In the bedroom, it is the bed that should be in the commanding position. Other rooms might require different pieces of furniture in the commanding

Tip: Give yourself a boost at school by sitting in the commanding position in your classrooms.

position, such as the couch in a living room or a desk in an office. The piece of furniture or activity placed in the commanding position will dominate the room. In China, most executives put their desks in the commanding position.

Desk and Computer

Computers and other major electronics are discouraged in the sanctuary of the bedroom. But many teens do share their bedrooms with a computer. This is not a problem as long as it's not adding so much yang energy as to disturb a sense of peace in the bedroom. A computer can be good in all guas as a source of electricity and energy. When working on your computer, try to sit with your back facing a wall so you can see the door. Do not face a wall or a corner unless you have no other option. If you must face a wall or corner, hang a mirror there so that you can see what is behind you and who enters.

Your computer is very good in the **Knowledge** gua if you intend to use it for learning, studying, doing homework, and creative writing. The **Family/Health** gua is also an excellent spot for a computer because the homework, focused attention, and serious study done here receives the support of your ancestors. If you hope to break away from family tradition or you frequently fight with your parents regarding college, work, or career choices, this is not where you'll want to place a workstation. A computer adds vitality to the **Wealth** gua, especially if you use your computer for financial information.

A computer is superb in the **Fame/Reputation** gua because the

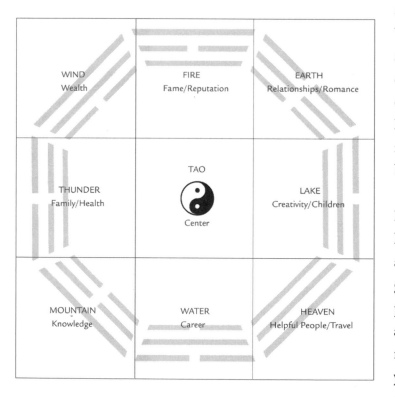

WIND
Wealth

FIRE
Fame/Reputation

EARTH
Relationships/Romance

THUNDER
Family/Health

TAO

Center

LAKE
Creativity/Children

MOUNTAIN
Knowledge

WATER
Career

HEAVEN
Helpful People/Travel

electrical energy adds vital chi. But mirrors are not good in this gua since their watery quality puts out the fire of fame (see chapter 13 for more detail), so you won't want to compensate with a mirror if you face the wall to be able to see the mouth of chi. If you must work with your back to the door in order to put your computer in this gua, it may be worthwhile to find a different location.

A computer is excellent in the **Creativity/Children** gua, especially if you use your computer for your creative self-expression such as writing or creating multimedia art. Your computer is good in the **Helpful people/ Travel** gua too, especially if you want to use it for networking, or finding grants, scholarships, and travel opportunities.

Dresser

A dresser can go in any gua. While dressers may not directly enhance a gua, they often provide surface area where favorite items such as jewelry or photos can be placed. What you keep on the top of your dresser may help you decide where you wish to place it. Jewelry goes particularly well in the **Wealth** gua, and photos work nicely in the **Family/Health** or **Relationships/Romance** guas. If you are limited by space and have just one option for your dresser, what you keep on top of your dresser should reflect the energy of that specific gua.

There are a few standards for dressers that apply no matter in which gua the dresser is placed:

❷ **Consider your dresser drawers similar to a mouth of chi** and keep them well oiled and aligned so it is easy to get in and out of them. Keep dresser drawers completely closed. Drawers that are misaligned, partially open, or closed but with fabric hanging out create sha chi. When dresser drawers are tightly closed, your clothes are protected and the chi of your room is less chaotic.

☯ Avoid milk crates and open containers for stacking clothes.
Improperly folded clothes on display create an immediate sense of disharmony. Anyone working in a retail clothing store can tell you that it takes too much energy to keep clothes neatly folded in a stack. Unless you are prepared to devote time and energy to folding your clothes in such a way that they appear neat and orderly, you will not want to use open-faced crates for clothing storage. And stacked milk crates tend to easily slide off one another, creating minor spills of clothing and awkward furniture lines that can result in poison arrows. Instead, try making shelves for a closet, if you have one, or pick up an inexpensive dresser at a garage sale or the Salvation Army. Make sure these used items have good chi.

Less Clothes, More Opportunity

As long as you're moving your dresser, take the opportunity to go through your clothing and personal items to decide what you are holding on to that is no longer appropriate for you. Get rid of these items to make space for the new things that will come your way. Rather than resist change, be open to it. Invite it. Create space for it, and welcome the new directions it will take you. One way to make a clothing purge fun is to include your friends. Plan a clothing swap party with your friends and have everyone bring the items they plan get rid of. Place all the clothes in the middle of a room and gleefully rummage. Make sure that at the end of the night everyone takes back any left-over stuff or make a group donation to a local thrift shop. You don't want to get stuck with everybody else's picked-over giveaways on top of your own.

- **If your dresser is really heavy and clunky, it could block the chi in the gua where it is located.** Move your dresser if you feel stuck in the life area that corresponds to your dresser placement.

Stereo Equipment

A stereo (or radio) can go in all eight gua locations because music and electricity bring energy and add chi. But which is the best gua for your stereo or radio? It depends on what you wish to accomplish and which area of your life you want to attract more energy to right now. If your stereo is also your alarm, you will probably want to place it within reaching distance of your bed. Below are the four best choices for stereo placement.

The **Creativity/Children** gua is perhaps the best location for a stereo or radio. You can connect easily with your favorite artists, and your own creativity is inspired. **Knowledge** is an excellent gua for your stereo or radio if you wish to learn about music and rhyme or to use music for meditation or as a healing tool. **Fame/Reputation** is a superb gua placement, especially if you are a musician, want to be known for your music, or plan to become a musician. Since most stereo equipment is black and the color red is the best for this gua, add red candles, red cloth, or some other red item. The **Career** gua is also superb for your stereo. The energy of your stereo's electricity and sound will enhance this gua and help your future career. If you are a musician or want to pursue a musical career, it is very helpful to place your stereo in this gua.

Bookshelves

Bookshelf placement will be determined by the items you store in them—presumably books. Books can support every area of your life and so bookshelves are appropriate in almost every gua. The only gua where they are not recommended is the Relationships/Romance gua since reading tends to be an introverted activity and the Relationships/Romance gua is about interacting with others.

When placing your bookshelves, take an extra minute to visit your books. Bookshelves are a haven for clutter. Do you have any books that would better serve you if you traded them in for credit at a used book store? Go through your books and sell or donate any book you have not touched in a year. The following guas are the best location for bookshelves.

The **Knowledge** gua is the very best location for all books because through books we learn and gain knowledge. It is highly recommended to place a bookshelf full of books in this corner gua. **Family/Health** is another superb gua for your books. Bookshelves are heavy so they add stability to your family. Photo albums and books that reflect your ancestry though history or literature go exceptionally well here. The **Creativity/Children** gua is a good place for your books since you can get very creative ideas from reading. But add the color white if your books are too dark in order to keep this an upbeat, yang gua. The **Helpful people/Travel** gua is an ideal spot for reference books such as dictionaries and almanacs.

TV

A TV is an electronic device that introduces a very yang element to your yin bedroom, so place it with caution. Though TVs are discouraged in the bedroom, if you must have one, it can go in practically any gua except the Relationships/Romance gua. You do not want your relationships to be with virtual people who do not really exist in your world. And people tend to watch far too much TV when it is placed in this gua.

Athletic Equipment

Athletic equipment is fine in almost any gua, but not if the equipment is broken. A broken Stairmaster, busted skis, old dance shoes, or weights that lie around unused will create heavy, stuck chi. You will block your own good fortune if weighed down by the very things that are supposed to be tools for your health. Where you place exercise equipment may depend on what type of exercise you are doing.

If your room is big enough, consider the **Knowledge** gua for exercise and movement that is meditative such as yoga or tai chi, or for keeping your yoga mat. The **Family/Health** gua is excellent for athletic equipment, especially for traditional sports such as baseball or activities that your family does together. The **Wealth** gua is generally not good for placement of athletic gear, as it can cause you to overspend on equipment. You might place your gear here temporarily if you want to raise money in an athletic event, such as a fund-raising marathon. If you are hoping for a career in sports, a sports scholarship, or accolades as an athlete, it is superb to place sports equipment in the **Fame/Reputation** or **Career** gua.

Avoid the **Relationships/Romance** gua for athletic equipment. If athletic equipment is placed here it could result in your relationships being like a workout and very draining. Broken equipment in the **Relationships/ Romance** gua is especially unfortunate. The one exception to avoiding the Relationships/Romance gua for athletic equipment is if you really enjoy working out and seek good friends with similar interests in sports.

Phone

While the phone isn't a physically large item, it is a prominent one. Fortunately, your phone is excellent in all guas because the ringing sound adds chi. Especially good is the **Relationships/Romance** gua and the **Helpful people/Travel** gua because the phone connects you with others. Arrange your phone wires so that they are neatly out of the way and no one can trip over them, which disrupts chi.

Consider Color

What's the least expensive thing you can do to dramatically transform a space? Change the colors that dominate your room. And what's the easiest way to this? Paint. Nothing will transform the chi of a room more quickly than a fresh coat of paint. A bedroom should emit yin energy for restful sleep, so white tones, soft pastel colors, or similar light colors are best for an overall room color. Stripes and patterns will create yang chi, so they are best avoided in the bedroom. Darker colors will tend to shrink a space, so use them sparingly.

Painting Your Room

Painting a room is a big project, but worth the payoff—a complete lifting of chi. (Keep in mind, though, that applying a new coat of paint usually requires advance permission from the owner of the space—be it a parent, school, or landlord.)

Types of Paint

If you are in the fortunate position of being able to paint your room, talk to someone at the paint or hardware store about the different kinds of paints. For indoor painting use water-based latex paints, not oil-based paints. Latex paints are the easiest to use and are better for the environment and your health.

Paint comes in three types of finishes: matte, semi-gloss, and gloss. Matte is not shiny and is best for the walls. Semi-gloss, also called satin, is a little shiny and is also good on walls. Gloss is very shiny and has the benefit of being very strong so it goes well on surfaces that are wiped down frequently, such as kitchen cabinets. Gloss and semi-gloss are frequently used for trims such as door frames, closet doors, and windowsills.

Saving Money on Paints

Color paint can be expensive. One way to cut cost is to have a friendly chat with an employee of your local hardware store. Often hardware stores keep paint in their back rooms, the results of custom color mixes that customers have asked for that didn't come out in the anticipated color. Smaller, local stores will often offer these paints to regular customers and artists at a discounted rate. There is usually nothing wrong with the paint other than the fact that it's not quite the color the previous customer wanted. Sometimes you can even find more original and creative hues than what's offered in the standard mixes.

The type of paint finish you select will affect the chi in your room. Too much glare will create sha chi (see page 22), so if your room already receives a lot of sunlight a matte finish is preferable since gloss reflects a lot of light. If your room is very dark consider a paint with a gloss finish to enhance light energy.

Preparing the Paint Surface

Before you start, you'll want to cover everything carefully, including the floor. Push as much as you can to the center of the room so that you are able to access all of the walls. Cover your possessions with a plastic tarp or cloth from the paint store. Put newspaper on the floor to capture any paint drips. Place thick masking tape around the borders of the surfaces you are painting to ensure clean, straight lines at the edges. Excess paint will drip on the tape rather than a neighboring surface. After the paint dries just pull the tape up and you'll have nice, clean lines.

You may need to wipe down the walls with a damp cloth so that the new paint won't go over spiderwebs or dirt. Also, take a moment to fill in any cracks in the plaster or holes in the Sheetrock. There are many products on the market that merely require a soft squeeze of a tube to release a caulk, glue, or filler that will seal up these chi leaks and make your walls look smoother and fresh. Most of these cost under ten dollars. Ask for help at your local hardware store for more painting information.

Ready, Set, Paint!

Once everything is covered and your painting surfaces are prepared, you're ready to paint. You can apply the paint with a brush or pour paint in a paint tray and use a roller, using a brush just to paint the edges. If you use a roller, paint the edges with a brush first and then use the roller to blend the brush strokes to avoid bumpy paint lines on your wall. Keep a damp cloth on hand to wipe up any wet paint drips or spills as you work.

Always paint with the windows open to avoid harmful exposure to those paint fumes. Spend the night at a friend's house or sleep in a different room until your walls are dry.

When you are done, be sure to dispose of your unused paint and clean up your brushes in an environmentally safe manner.

If you can't get permission to paint or don't have time or energy right now you can freshen up your room with a good wipe down of the walls with a sponge. And you can add color to any gua with objects such as pillows, posters, or books.

Don't Forget the Lights!

Your lighting will have major impact on the balance of chi in your room. Light can be a primary factor in determining how yang or yin a space feels. Remember the chart you filled out on pages 10 and 11? What type of

Feng Shui Color Guide

It you want to attract a particular kind of energy into your life, consider painting an associated color on trim, a door, or a small wall. You can use the chart below to guide your choice of colors for painting accents and trim.

Blue: Yin. This is a good color for the Knowledge gua. Blue represents blessings and is a calming, peaceful color for meditation and contemplation.

Red: Yang. This is the best color for the Fame/Reputation gua. It is symbolic of virtue and truth. Red wards off evil and its vibrancy is life affirming. It is the color of life, luck, prosperity, power, glory, and happiness.

Green: Yang. This is the best color for the Family/Health gua. Green symbolizes hope, longevity, and vitality. It represents lush growth, vegetation, and the rebirth of springtime.

Purple: Yin. This is the best color for the Wealth gua. Purple has a function similar to red and can be used with red and gold to symbolize wealth. Purple is associated with royalty and pageantry.

Pink: Yin. As a combination of red and white, pink is best in the Relationships/Romance gua.

White: Yang. This is the best color for the Creativity/Children gua, for white represents spiritual and moral purity.

Gray: Yin. Gray goes well in the Helpful people/Travel gua. Gray—composed of black and white—is a color of connection.

Black: Yang. Black or deep blue is the best color for the Career gua, as it symbolizes seriousness and justice. It is also the color of deep waters and the darkness of winter. Black is not usually considered lucky, but when used in balance with other colors it can absorb negative chi.

Yellow: Yang. This is a good color for the center of the ba-gua, such as a rug in the center of the room. Yellow can indicate authority or rank and it is associated with tolerance, acceptance, honesty, and trustworthiness.

Gold: Yin. Like yellow, gold is good at the center of the ba-gua. It is a symbol of wealth and prosperity.

lighting do you like best? To determine the kind of lighting you want in your bedroom, pay attention to how other houses and places are lit. Some basic considerations for lighting are:

- **The lightbulb choice.** Lightbulbs come in different colors and brightness. They also offer different types of light, such as fluorescent as opposed to incandescent. The brighter your lightbulb, the more yang you add to an environment. Rarely use red lighting in a bedroom because it is too yang, although a red light can be used in a social room like a den or living room. For the bedroom, the best lighting is soft, relaxing natural light. Most hardware stores now sell energy-efficient lightbulbs that offer the effect of natural daylight.

- **The style of lamp.** Teen bedrooms are the perfect place for lamps that allow you to adjust the lighting intensity. For example, when you have friends in your room, you can increase yang by having the lights at full force. When it's time to relax and get ready for bed, you can bring the energy down with nice, soft lighting.

- **Location of the light source.** Lights create chi, so you can aim them where you want to direct energy. A ceiling light in the center of the room is a good source of chi for the entire room. If you have slanted ceilings in a gua, you can aim a light so it reflects off the slanted ceiling, compensating for the loss of chi brought about by the shorter wall. Sunlight that comes into a room through windows is the best possible source of light, as long as it's not overwhelming.

Window Coverings

Windows allow light to enter a room, which adds chi to the space. But at night, a window can become like a black hole that sucks energy out. Window coverings are important to prevent this black hole effect. Even if bright lights are outside your window, you'll want to close off that yang energy to experience peaceful sleep.

Venetian blinds are not good feng shui because they make a shadow pattern like knife blades, creating poison arrows. If you live in a drafty house in a cold area, choose shades that have some insulation or are lined to keep in the heat. Unfortunately, most insulated window coverings block the light altogether, creating an excess of yin. Try to compensate for this with a nice yang white color. If you live in a warmer climate, you have many options for window coverings. Consider matching your curtains to the color of the gua in which that window is located (see graphic below). Hang curtains of a solid shade or a soft pattern that is not too busy or chaotic. (See page 185–187 to learn more about how window coverings impact the yin-yang factor of your room.)

In all cases, make sure your windows aren't cracked, broken, or dirty. Any of these three conditions will block the flow of chi.

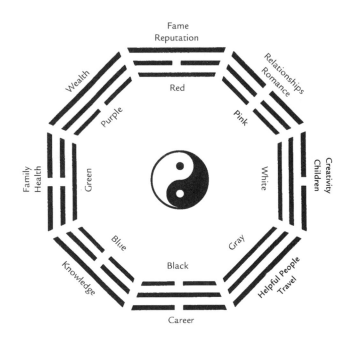

ACTIVITY: CREATE YOUR DESIGN SCHEME

Things you'll need:

• The ba-gua map of your room that you created in the activity on pages 38–39

• Pencil, tape, scissors, ruler

• Tape measure or yardstick

• $\frac{1}{4}$-inch graph paper or the $\frac{1}{4}$-inch grid on the next page

Each square on the grid or graph paper equals 1 foot. Measure the length and width of your room and draw a square or rectangle (or whatever the actual shape is) of that many feet on your paper. Using the ba-gua map you made of your room, mark the eight areas of your life.

Measure your bed. Using $\frac{1}{4}$ inch to equal 1 foot, measure and cut out a piece of colored paper or graph paper to represent your bed. Label it "Bed."

Do the same for any other big pieces of furniture you have like your desk, bookshelf, stereo shelf, dresser, or athletic equipment.

Review the information provided in this chapter to pick good locations for each major item and place the cutouts on your "room" in the guas where you think they will go best.

Do they all fit? If not, rearrange them, giving highest priority to the location of the bed. Then consult the information in this chapter to find good alternative locations for things that overlap.

Satisfied? Then tape all the cutouts on your paper or draw them in. If you want to paint, write down the color or colors and types of paint you would like to use. Now you have the basic design of your new room.

You probably have many small items that have yet to be placed. As you turn through the pages of part 3, you will learn more about the nature of the eight areas of life and what types of objects go well in each gua. As you refine your intentions for your life and each corresponding gua, continue to use this design scheme. Write in the small items as you discover where they belong and change the locations of the larger items if need be to suit your personal goals.

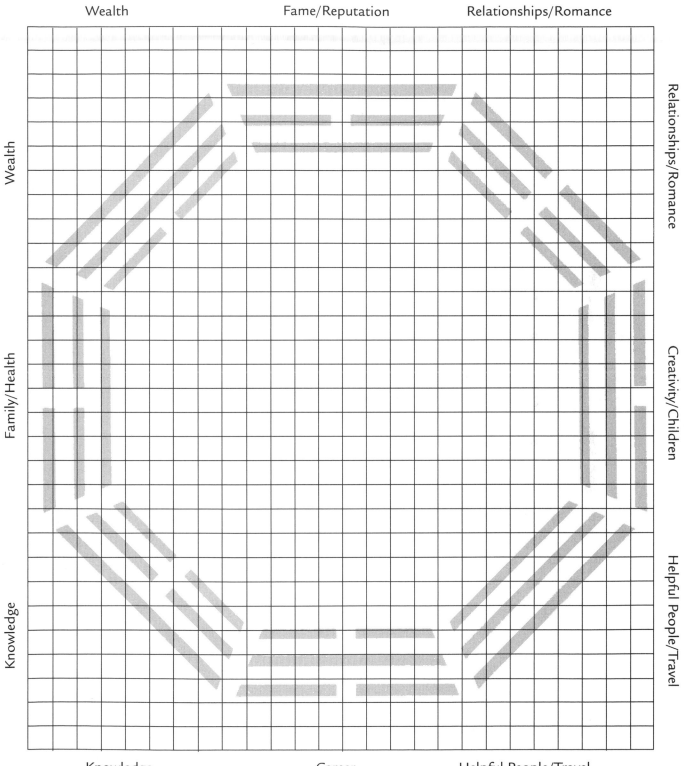

It's Your Move

Once you cleared away the clutter, opened up your mouth of chi, and created space to move around in, you will immediately feel the increase in the positive chi energy in your room. Now that you've figured out what colors you want to use and where the big items will go, it's time to move around your furniture to match your design scheme. Keep in mind that you will continue to rearrange items as you read through parts 3 and 4 to refine your feng shui skills and clarify your life goals. If you are uncertain about the placement of a particular item it's okay to hold off. Find a temporary location for it while you continue to read the rest of this book.

If you need help moving the big items, consider asking a friend or two to lend a hand. Maybe you could return the favor and help them arrange their rooms according to feng shui.

The final step in moving your large items is a good cleaning up of the dust revealed from all the movement of furniture and objects. A good way to remove dust is to run a slightly moist rag over the surfaces of your room, such as tabletops, dresser tops, and windowsills. Use a rag that is moist enough to catch the dust but not so moist as to leave stains. Finally, vacuum or sweep the floor. Give yourself a few moments to sit back and experience the circulation of good energy in your room. AHHHH!

Part Three

The Eight
Areas of
Your Life

ou have purged your world of things that no longer suit you and found a respectful storage place for those things that you wish to keep but no longer need to see every day. You have placed the major items of furniture in your room in the areas where they do not block the mouth of chi. The next step is to fine-tune what goes where. This can be the most rewarding part of feng shui. Your room is your opportunity to create your own sense of identity.

As you delve more into feng shui, consider your intentions. Intention is a primary part of what makes feng shui work. By focusing your intentions through object placement in your room, you are reminded of your life priorities. The act of moving and placing objects becomes a ritual that concretizes and adds density to your will. This is where feng shui becomes personalized and your room becomes about you.

As you go through these chapters, focus on what each gua means to you and what your personal intention is for each gua. Who are you and what energies are you hoping to attract in your life? These are the questions that are answered as you begin to take charge of your space and arrange

Intention:
A determination to act in a certain way.
—*Webster's Dictionary*

it in a way that suits you and is in alignment with the principles of nature.

Note: As you continue to refine your design scheme you will find that not all items will fit exactly where you'd like to place them. Fortunately, most items have at least three or four guas into which they may be appropriately placed. When in doubt, consult the Eight Areas of Your Life Activity that you filled out on page 16 and use your rating system to help you prioritize which guas are the most important to you. Make sure that those areas contain objects that support your goals.

To see your wishes in your mind and make them come true, you have to be right minded. Do good things for others without expecting a return. Having a good heart is the road to achieving what your heart desires. It's a cycle that increases upon itself.

—DR. BAOLIN WU, FROM *LIGHTING THE EYE OF THE DRAGON*

5

Knowledge: Mountain

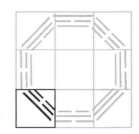

The Knowledge area of your room is located in the left corner near the door, the mouth of chi. This area represents all kinds of knowledge: facts and information, scholastic study, self knowledge, and universal wisdom. The Knowledge gua is associated with Mountain; when we cultivate self-awareness, we can be as solid, secure, and immovable as a mountain.

Knowledge can be found in books and classes, magazines and newspapers, the Internet and radio, meditation and mental exercises, literature and poetry, art, and nature. Knowledge can be found virtually anywhere, if you know how to seek it. Information, debate, dialogue, and curiosity are gifts that allow us to be passionately involved in learning and self-betterment.

In school, we are often bombarded by facts that we are expected to memorize and process. It's easy to believe that knowledge is about acquiring and retaining as much information as possible. Yet this is just one of many forms of knowledge. The *Tao Te Ching* tells us

> Knowing others is intelligence.
> Knowing yourself is true wisdom.
> Mastering others is strength.
> Mastering yourself is true power.

An aspect of knowing yourself is discovering what inspires your internal love of learning—whether it be learning about car engines or foreign languages—and establishing a lifelong relationship of curiosity between yourself and the world. How do you learn? Are you someone who retains information best if you read it, or do you prefer conversations? Or are you very visual and learn best by watching and observing? Do you work best at a formal desk, or are you more comfortable reading in a big chair? Do you like lots of quiet (yin) when you study or do you like to be in a loud café (yang)? Most of all, what inspires you? Where are your curiosities? What do you seek to know?

A happy life is one which is in accordance with its own nature.
—SENECA

Use the answers to these questions to arrange the Knowledge gua of your room. Most people place a desk and/or bookshelves in this gua. But before you do so, take a moment to think about what knowledge means to you. Think about your favorite learning environment, and then ask yourself what you can do to evoke the same atmosphere in your own room. Some people might pick a library environment with an old oak desk for a sense of formal study and structure. Others might prefer a lounge chair and funky reading lamp for a flowing, relaxed environment in which they can open their mind to new ideas.

You can learn to know others through observation, books, art, film, and various forms of study. You can hear the wisdom of previous generations through poetry, stories, scriptures, and music. You can explore the physical

The Master said, "Yu, have you ever been told of the six sayings about the six degenerations?" Tzu-lu replied, "No, never." [The Master said] "Come, then; I will tell you. The love of being benevolent without the love of learning leads to foolish simplicity. The love of knowing without the love of learning leads to dissipation of the mind. The love of being sincere without the love of learning leads to a disregard of consequences. The love of straightforwardness without the love of learning leads to rudeness. The love of boldness without the love of learning leads to insubordination. The love of firmness without the love of learning leads to extravagant conduct."

—ADAPTED FROM CONFUCIUS'S
THE ANALECTS, BOOK XVII

world or exercise your mind through math, science, or philosophy. You can engage in the dialogue of our contemporary time by reading essays, magazines, and newspapers. But it is how you integrate these facts, histories, and mental practices into your own life experience, into your own soul's journey, that sets the course of your own personal knowing and discovery of inner wisdom.

In order to develop a sense of self-knowledge and get in touch with your inner wisdom, Taoists recommend doing the same thing you do when you apply feng shui to your room: remove clutter.

> *Empty your mind of all thoughts.*
> *Let your heart be at peace.*
> *Watch the turmoil of beings,*
> *but contemplate their return.*
> —LAO-TZU, FROM THE *TAO TE CHING*

We are bombarded daily with information—through television, news, school, music, and advertising. This turns into mental noise that can become like clutter, gathering in the recesses of our mind and taking up space where other forms of knowledge might manifest. Just as we remove clutter to create better harmony and flow in our living space, we must remove the clutter in our minds in order to hear our own inner truths and discover our wisdom.

You can learn to stop the mental clutter with silence, learning to hear your wordless inner voice. In Zen Buddhism, meditation can lead you into a state called *satori,* the realm where the knower is the known, a place of oneness with the universe. Mystics, shamans, and philosophers have different names and descriptions for this state of profound connection with our primal selves. It is always there, and even without hours of meditation we touch into our inner silence and have small moments of enlightenment every day.

ACTIVITY: DEFINING YOUR INTENTIONS

Use the lines below to write down your intentions for the Knowledge gua of your room: What atmosphere do you seek to create for your optimal learning environment?

_____

_____

_____

_____

_____

_____

_____

_____

What to Put in the Knowledge Gua

The Knowledge area of your room is your personal place for reflection and self-development. This is an ideal area to create a place to sit, read, relax, and meditate. Make sure this area is not cluttered; a cluttered Knowledge area parallels a cluttered mind.

Bookcase: This is the best location for the bookcase (see the discussion on pages 59–60).

Altar: This is a superb gua for situating any kind of personal altar. Some people dedicate small altars to their faith, with images of Christ, Kwan Yin, ancient Goddesses, Buddha, Krishna, or other deities. Other people choose to avoid deities and, instead, create a small altar for objects that inspire a sense of well-being: special rocks, a plant, pictures of friends and family, a vase of live flowers, or candles. Altars can be constructed easily using small tables covered by cloth.

Tools for self-discovery: Books, tarot cards and materials for other oracle practices, journals, and self-expressive art are excellent in this area.

Pictures and posters: This is a good area for pictures or posters of persons or objects that represent knowledge and wisdom for you. This gua corresponds to mountains in Chinese philosophy, so a poster of mountains or flowers that inspire peace and contemplation are also good here. If you must hang posters of the dark side or Goth images in your room, place them here so you can learn about the shadowy side of life and why you are attracted to it.

Hobbies: This is a very good gua for learning about yourself and expressing yourself through your hobby. It is also good for understanding more about your hobby.

Your True Self

Throughout our lives we are identified by our statistics—name, hair color, age, skin color, and cultural background. But is that you? Are you still you if your hair color changes or you grow a year older? Who is the person who dreams at night? Who is the one who imagines things? Which you is you?

While people will identify you by external factors like name and age, fewer people will ever name you by your internal qualities: "There goes the one who speaks quietly to small animals." Is it so surprising that we don't always take the time to name and identify the subtle parts of ourselves? Yet these quiet, unnamed parts of ourselves have enormous influence over our actions and choices.

Here's something to think about: You will spend more time with yourself than anyone else on this planet—more than a parent, more than a sibling, more than a spouse or child. How many hours a day do you spend talking with friends or examining relationships with other people? Now, how many hours do you spend talking with yourself and examining that relationship? Does something seem a little out of proportion? The Knowledge gua of your room is a special place where you can spend time with yourself and gain insight into who you are and who you want to become.

> To be nobody-but-yourself—in a world which is doing its best, night and day, to make you everybody else—means to fight the hardest battle which any human being can fight; and never stop fighting.
>
> —E. E. CUMMINGS

Ways to Self-knowledge

There are many ways to explore the world of self-knowledge. Some of these include:

- **Pay attention to your thoughts.** When you look in the mirror, what kinds of things do you say to yourself? Do you give yourself positive

GETTING TO KNOW YOURSELF—A KNOWLEDGE QUIZ

Use these questions to reflect on who you are, what you believe, and who you want to become. Write your answers and date the page so you can see how you change over time, and how you change after you apply feng shui to your room.

Date:_____

What do I know about myself right now?

_____

If someone asked me to describe myself, I would say:

_____

Right now, the thing I want most in my life is:

_____

My favorite music is:

_____

One thing I've never tried but would like to is:

_____

Activities that are really important to me are:

_____

I take care of myself by:

_____

I choose my clothing style because:

_____

My ideal world would be:

_____

I wish:

_____

The thing I'm most afraid of is:

_____

I believe God is:

_____

I feel really good when:

_____

Someone I deeply respect is:

_____

I aspire to:

_____

feedback and support, or do you criticize every stumble and focus on every mistake? The difference between a relationship with yourself and a relationship with your friends is that your friends will let you know when you've hurt their feelings or will support you when you're down. We can't always hear our own selves enough to know if we have hurt our own feelings. Nor can we always hear the inner voice that supports us. Just like any other friend, you have a lot to learn from yourself. How are you treating yourself these days?

☯ **Keep a dream diary.** Examining your dreams is a magical way to discover what's going on inside your head and heart. There are many different books and theories about how to interpret dreams, but the best dream interpretation is the personal meaning that you feel most deeply. Regardless of what meaning you attach to your dreams, in order to interpret them, you first need to remember them. Keeping a dream diary will help you develop the capacity to remember your dreams. Keep a simple notebook by the side of your bed and record your dreams as soon as you wake up, before you even get out of bed. At first, you may just remember little things: "I think so-and-so was in my dream last night . . ." Write it down anyway and include the date. If you can't even remember much, that's okay. Start out with a simple description of how you woke up feeling: "I feel refreshed, but I can't remember my dreams" or "I feel like I didn't sleep at all last night, I'm so tired." Try doing this for a week and see what happens. Soon you'll start recalling more and more details about your dreams, until you recapture entire story lines.

☯ **Use oracles and divination tools.** Tarot, I Ching, and runes are some common forms of divination. Each of these systems has a unique way of allowing us to get in touch with our intuitive (yin) side. The use of oracular and symbolic language allows us to formulate interpretations of the world around us. In its simplest form, divination can be as easy as asking the universe for a sign. On a more complex level, the symbols of the tarot cards, I Ching, or runes can inspire our subconscious knowledge about ourselves and the energy around us. Whatever your chosen form of divination, the more you work with a particular oracle, the more powerful and precise it will become.

- **Meditate.** Blaise Pascal, French philosopher and scientist, once stated, "All human evil comes from a single cause: man's inability to sit still in a room." Most of us find ourselves encouraged to be in a constant state of activity—school, sports, meal preparation, socializing, hobbies, community involvement, and jobs. Meditation encourages us to put aside all of this external noise to discover what it is to be truly still. There are many different forms of meditation. One of the more common forms of meditation consists of sitting still for fifteen to thirty minutes, gently keeping your head and spine straight, while focusing on your breath moving in and out. Or you can concentrate on a mantra, a special word, repeated with each breath. These and many other meditation techniques encourage us to calm our over-active minds and help us attain the inner quiet and stillness that connects us with our primal identity, our deepest reality. Here is where knowledge begins.

> All human evil comes from a single cause: man's inability to sit still in a room.
>
> —Blaise Pascal

- **Keep a journal.** By writing down your inner thoughts and feelings, you can learn many fascinating things about yourself, and even write your way to wisdom. Journal writing is private, just for you. The kind of writing you do for school may or may not be what your soul requires for expansion and enlightenment—you do it because you have to. But what you write in your journal, unlike homework, is your own soul taking flight, your own journey to knowledge. Through writing you can process your day, explore your dreams and desires, organize your thoughts, and witness your self-development.

A Simple Meditation Technique

Sit on the floor with your legs crossed "Indian style" and your back straight. Keep your ears, shoulders, and hips in a straight line. Rest your palms face up on your knees. Close your eyes three-quarters of the way, keeping your visual focus on the floor about one foot in front of you. Once you are in a comfortable position and your body is still, bring your attention to your breath. Feel your breath going in and out. Begin to count one full count for each inhale and each exhale. Slow your breathing and keep focused on your breath. If you are very still, in time you will hear another sound—the sound of your heartbeat. Any time a thought comes up, imagine it placed in a cloud and watch it float away. As your thoughts surface from "Am I doing this right?" or "What do I want for dinner?"—just let these thoughts pass like clouds. After a few weeks of gently meditating each day, you can discover a lot about your thoughts. With our thoughts we create the world.

☯ **Go to counseling.** Sometimes we need the help of others to guide us to our true selves. Counseling often has a bad reputation as something only crazy, weak, or self-indulgent people do. This is not the case. Counseling can be an excellent tool for self-understanding. It is used by all sorts of people, from every profession and every walk of life. There are many different types of counseling. Should you choose counseling as a tool for self-exploration, it's important that both the counselor and his or her method feel right for you. Some people are much more comfortable with a lot of conversation and dialogue with their counselor. Others prefer to talk and have their counselor listen. Regardless of the style, a counselor should be someone you feel you can trust, and someone who respects you for the wonderful, unique, complex, and powerful individual that you are.

Additional Resources

The Complete Tarot Kit by Susan Levitt will help you learn how to read the tarot for yourself.

I Ching for Teens by Julie Tallard Johnson is an easy-to-follow guide to using the I Ching as an oracle.

Peace Is Every Step: The Path of Mindfulness in Everyday Life by Thich Nhat Han explains how to achieve a mindful approach to all aspects of your life.

Please Understand Me by David Keirsey and Marilyn Bates will help you discover your personality type through a popular quiz based on Freudian psychology.

Twenty Questions: An Introduction to Philosophy by G. Lee Bowie, Meredith W. Michaels, and Robert C. Solomon, eds., combines samples of classic philosophical essays with works by poets, novelists, journalists, and politicians to inspire exploration of life's major themes, from "what is art?" to "who am I?"

6

Family/Health: Thunder

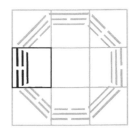

The Family/Health area of your room is located in the center of the wall on your left when you enter your room. This area represents how you relate to your parents, siblings, and other relatives. The Family/Health gua also represents your health, since most health problems run in the family. The Family/Health gua is associated with thunder. Our ancestors precede us as thunder precedes a storm. Conscious attention to this gua can transform conflicting family relationships into experiences of gratitude, mutual respect, and appreciation for our parents, ancestors, and teachers. This area also corresponds to the balance of power with bosses and managers at work.

Here is where you focus to improve the connection you have with your family—to resolve family problems and conflicts, to live more harmoniously with sisters and brothers, and to improve your physical health and well-being. If you live with guardians or in a foster home or group home, the people you live with are considered family. Your extended family includes grandparents, aunts, uncles, cousins, ancestors, even family pets. Keep this area clean to keep your family strong and unified. This area also influences your family's fate.

The Family Hierarchy

For thousands of years during several Chinese empires, family roles were clearly defined according to a traditionally accepted hierarchy. The writings of the great Chinese sage Confucius (c. 551–479 B.C.) offered rules of conduct to encourage harmony and balance for all types of relationships. Even where to sit at the dining room table was decided by an individual's place within the family hierarchy.

In the arrangement below the father sits in the commanding position at the far end of the table, deepest into the dining room and facing the entrance. In contemporary times, rules of conduct for family members are changing and evolving. Not everyone lives in a family with both parents. Often the role of family power and responsibility is assumed by a single

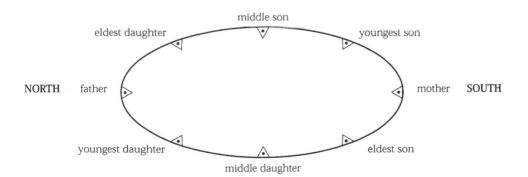

Confucius instructed that there was a natural order to the family. Maintaining this order in settings such as the dining room table shown here promotes harmony and balance.

What to Put in the Family/Health Gua

- **Family photographs:** Images of family unity (such as large family portraits) or happy moments with family members are ideal for this gua (see the activity on page 91).

- **Heirlooms:** Jewelry, medals, furniture, and other special objects handed down from grandparents or other relatives are great for the Family/Health gua.

- **Altar to your ancestors:** Family heirlooms and objects that represent your sense of cultural identity go well here.

- **Green:** Enhance this gua with dashes of all shades of green, from light mint pastels to deep forest green.

- **Plants:** Lush plants add chi to any gua and can be a wonderful way to add green to this area. As the plant grows, the family grows. If a plant withers or dies, replace it to maintain the good health of those in your family.

- **Vitamins and medicine:** If you keep vitamins, prescription medicine, birth control, or medicinal herbs in your bedroom, this is where you will want to store them.

- **Body products:** Anything that supports your health and your healthy relationship to your body will naturally work in the Family/Health gua. Bath salts and body lotions go nicely here, as does bottled water.

- **Exercise equipment:** If you have enough space, this is a good gua for exercise equipment, weights, and a yoga mat.

What *Not* to Put in the Family/Health Gua

- **Vices:** This gua is a focal point for sustaining good health, so avoid placing any items here that create ill health, such as recreational drugs, diet pills, or junk food. Many vices may encourage illness or addiction if placed in the Family/Health gua.

mother. In these cases it may be most appropriate that the mother, or the person who demonstrates a leadership role in the family, sits in the commanding position at the table.

Balance and Harmony in the Family

How each of us relates to our parents varies drastically from person to person. Your parents may be like close and understanding friends. Or perhaps your parents are controlling or strict. Relationships with parents during the teen years can be confusing and tricky. Small children need direct guidance and supervision from adults in order to develop and safely maneuver their way through the world. But as a teen, your journey is to begin to learn how to guide and supervise yourself. By doing so, you break out of the habits of your parent/child relationship and form an entirely new way of relating to your parents and to other adults around you.

Sometimes the adults in your life might resist these shifts. You have spent every year of your childhood aware that you are growing and developing through changes in age, grade, and shoe size. But your parents may be so focused on helping you grow and change that they've forgotten they must do so as well.

As the changing, growing teen, you are a force of chi within your family unit. By growing from a child to an adult, you are shifting family dynamics. Your parents are no longer the only adult voices in the household. Younger siblings may lose you as a playmate but gain an older mentor. Older siblings may lose a child's adoring attention and instead gain a peer, or perhaps a competitor. According to the Tao, all things must change. Conflict will occur if others respond to the changing chi of your teen years with resistance. Assist yourself and others to accept these changes by using images of positive transformation as decoration in your room, on your notebooks and screensavers, and other places where you exercise creative control. Images of butterflies, cocoons, budding seeds, and sunrises can be peaceful reminders that, while all things change, we need not fear change.

Sharing Your Room with a Sibling or Roommate

If you share a room with someone else, you probably won't have the same amount of freedom to create your feng shui environment. If you are lucky, your roommate shares your interest in feng shui, and together you can have fun reviewing the eight guas and deciding what you wish to place in them. But if you don't see eye to eye in this way, you can maintain an invisible boundary to mark where your space in the room begins. It is possible for you to create a mouth of chi and discern where the eight areas fit into your part of the room without impacting your roommate's space. Such arrangements are less than ideal, but you can still begin your feng shui journey. Don't be surprised if your roommate becomes interested in feng shui after you elevate the chi.

Following are some general considerations for shared rooms. You'll have to be creative in applying these tips to your room and specific situation.

Bed Position When You Share a Room

If you share your bedroom with another person, the one whose bed is deeper in the room has more power and has the advantage. For balance, maybe you and your roommate can change bed positions every six months. If you share a room with a much younger sibling, your bed should be in the commanding position. You can then place your younger siblings bed in the Creativity/Children gua because it is also the gua for children.

Bunk Beds

Bunk beds are not considered good feng shui because the person on the lower bunk has less air circulation and is sleeping under the weight of the person in the top bunk. This can have adverse effects on the health of the person in

ACTIVITY: FAMILY PHOTO COLLAGE

The Family/Health gua is a great place to keep family photos. Charge this gua by making a photo collage for your wall containing the pictures of your relatives: grandparents, parents, siblings, cousins, aunts, uncles, and special people whom you consider family. If you have images of great-grandparents and other elders, include them too. If you don't have pictures of everybody, or prefer to be creative, you can represent individuals with their name surrounded in a design of your choice. If you have a family crest or a symbol from ancestral homelands, you may choose to place this in the center of the collage.

Some people might choose to design their collage in the form of a family tree, with the ancestors at the roots and subsequent generations springing up as branches and leaves. Another option is to arrange the family members in a circle, following Confucious's order of the balanced placement of family members shown on page 87.

the lower bunk and can create an imbalance of power in the relationship between the two bunk mates. If you must have bunk beds, you can lift the chi of the lower bunk by decorating the bottom of the upper bed with light colors, or painting it with a sky motif such as clouds or a map of the planets, or any other images that indicate open, expansive space. You can also hang a tiny bell from the bottom of the top bunk to lift the chi. Be sure to choose a bell that makes a sound you enjoy hearing. Ring the bell often to move energy around, perhaps once every time you enter or leave the bed.

Creating Boundaries

There are many ways to divide a space. The first consideration to create boundaries in a room is checking in with the person with whom you are creating the boundary. If you start sectioning off a shared room without talking to the other person, the boundary will be perceived with hostility. Rather than coming across as you asserting your need for privacy and independence, your efforts will come across as a direct attempt to take away space from another person and shut them out from your life. The resulting resentment can grow into very negative energy being constantly flung in your direction. Such tension can easily be avoided by bringing the roommate into the boundary-making process. Chances are that person would appreciate the opportunity to have some space of their own as well.

A good way to divide boundaries is by using a folding screen. Folding screens consisting of three panels can serve as a wall without limiting light. A row of medium-height plants can also be used to create friendly boundaries. Make sure the plants are healthy and have round leaves, not plants with sharp, pointy leaves or protrusions. Some people like to create a pleasant atmosphere by stringing small white lights ("Christmas tree lights") inside the tall plants. This also helps define a boundary while lifting the chi. Just keep the electric wires tidy. It is not recommended to hang fabric from the ceiling to create a partition. The fabric wall will be insubstantial and will billow from any movement. Instead, use ceiling or floor lights, carpets, and plants to define your space. Arrange your lighting so that a ceiling fixture aims light into the center of your part of the room. Fortify that center with an area rug. The combination of a ceiling light and area rug will attract chi to the center of your part of the room.

A Word on Health

Chinese medicine seeks to balance and enhance the flow of chi inside the body. Chinese medical theory follows the same principles of yin and yang and elemental balance as applied in the art and science of feng shui. Chinese are renowned for the success of their ancient healing and lifestyle practices that result in vibrant health and longevity. Choosing a lifestyle that supports the health of your body can improve not only the length of your life, but also the quality of it. A healthy body is more capable of clear thinking, positive emotions, and energetic achievements.

Being kind to your health can also be quite luxurious and can include such practices as aromatherapy, massage, baths, and exercise. Exercise means different things to different people. If you have a lot of Fire or Wood elements in your composition, you might prefer the rush of fast, competitive, team sports, such as basketball or soccer. If you have more Earth or Water elements, you might find you enjoy quiet activities that are less team-oriented, such as biking, swimming, or hiking. (See pages 159–167 for a quiz on your elements.) Identifying the form of exercise you enjoy can be one of the best lifestyle gifts you can give yourself. If you are constantly trying to force yourself to go for a jog, but would much rather be walking and chatting to a friend, consider giving up jogging and going for long walks. You're more likely to take better care of your body by walking a little every day than by running half-heartedly once a week while berating yourself the whole time for being out of shape. If you love team sports and robust activity, you might find that not getting enough of this kind of activity throughout the course of the day will lead you to become restless and agitated. Try new types of exercise and movement until you discover the ones that flow best with who you are.

A Healthy Symbol

In China the turtle represents good health and longevity. If your Family/Health gua needs a simple lift, try charging it with turtle images. A small turtle sculpture or picture of a turtle works well here. So would a live turtle, as long as you maintain the turtle's health and keep the turtle's living environment clean and fresh.

The Eight Branches of Chinese Medicine

Feng shui is one of eight branches of Chinese medicine. How can we heal or enjoy good health if we are in a cluttered environment? All of the eight branches of Chinese medicine blend together to improve and sustain the health of our bodies, our spirits, our energy, and happiness in all areas of our life. The eight branches of Chinese medicine are:

- **Feng shui:** How to create a balanced and harmonious environment.

- **Meditation:** How to focus your mind and create peace and joy in your heart.

- **Exercise:** How to use exercise to feel more stable and centered and to defend yourself from danger.

- **Diet:** How to know which foods are healthy for you and how to select foods according to season and climate.

- **Herbology:** How to use Chinese herbs to heal ailments, gain strength, and cure specific health problems, such as headaches, painful menstruation, acne, and much more.

- **Astrology:** How to understand the cycles of the heavens and their influence on earth, using the Chinese lunar calendar, Chinese animal birth signs, and Chinese animal years. (Astrology is discussed further in chapter 15.)

- **Massage:** How to use healing touch to enhance health and cultivate chi flow in the body to prevent disease.

- **Acupuncture:** How to use the art and science of inserting fine needles into chi points in the body to open the body's flow and unblock stagnation.

Vices or Experimentation?

Few people get out of their teen years without experimenting with some vice. Typical vices that you might encounter include smoking, drinking, chewing tobacco, taking narcotics, binge eating, shoplifting, excessive sexual experimentation, and even experimenting with self-mutilation. While each of these vices may have a particular meaning in the life of the person engaging in them, they also come with consequences—economic, social, and physical.

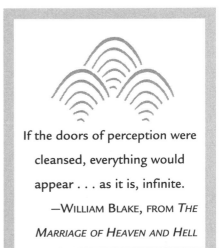

If the doors of perception were cleansed, everything would appear . . . as it is, infinite.
—WILLIAM BLAKE, FROM *THE MARRIAGE OF HEAVEN AND HELL*

The habits you form in your teenage years can shape and direct the rest of your life. Only you can decide if you want to develop vices and carry them with you into your adult years. Remember that habitual behaviors can become like clutter on your shelves, blocking new opportunities. You can invite chi into your life by periodically examining your behaviors and revisiting whether or not they still have a use in your life. If they are no longer serving you, then they are clutter and they must go. If they are preventing you from achieving other goals or engaging in other activities, they are blocking your good fortune. If vices are seeping into your life and affecting your work, school, family, and health, reconsider the importance you've given them in your life.

Part of this process includes becoming conscious of marketing manipulations. Companies and individuals who financially profit from other people's vices invest a lot of money in seducing consumers. Cigarette companies funnel millions of dollars into advertising campaigns. Alcohol companies do the same. If you've chosen to avoid these vices, friends engaged in them may encourage you to begin these behaviors in order to validate their own choice. In the face of such pressures, you'll have to choose over and over again whether or not you will buy in to the hype.

If you wish to avoid the trappings of vices, you might need to actively strategize. First, take a look around your room. Are there any images that are counter to your efforts to stay healthy? Musicians smoking? Airbrushed models promoting an unnatural expectation for your body type? An artistic advertisement that happens to be promoting alcohol? Take them all down. Find an image of the musician without a cigarette. Find sketches of fashion designs that just feature clothes. Replace advertising with authentic art. Create an environment that supports you.

The energy and desire to engage in a vice comes from chi imbalance. If you find yourself engaging in vices, consider using Taoist principles of energy to redirect destructive behavior into positive habits. The following chart offers helpful alternatives.

If you are having problems with vices and addiction, the most important gua to develop is your Helpful people/Travel gua. Find people with whom you feel safe talking about your habits. Experimentation with vices is common, but if you're experimenting, it helps to have feedback from someone who understands the risks of behavior and can keep an eye on you to make sure you are safe. Finding help to better understand and remove whatever chronic discomfort or pain that may be leading to experimentation that has become self-destructive is the appropriate and mature thing to do.

HABIT	ALTERNATIVE ACTIVITIES	SUPPORTING FENG SHUI ACTIVITY
Smoking	Breathing, meditating, exercising, singing	Fortify your bedroom (which represents the lungs of the house) with aromatherapy that will expand your breathing and encourage your interest in healing with scent. Eucalyptus and pine are the scents that strongly support the health of the lungs.
Alcohol	Taking baths, painting, writing, poetry, using divination, creating rituals, working with crystals	Alcohol consumption is closely associated with family patterns. Focus on peaceful colors for your Family/Health gua: Azure blue or green are highly recommended. Place a chime in this gua and energize the chi by ringing it often.
Narcotics	Drumming, dancing, pursuing yang sports such as skateboarding and snowboarding	Narcotics are associated with the element of Fire, which corresponds to your Fame/Reputation gua (see chapter 8). Clear off the walls of your Fame/Reputation gua. Place one simple image of powerful art that is red, the fiery color of power. Charge your Creativity/Children gua with white flowers.
Unhealthy Eating	Gardening, practicing yoga, weight lifting, knitting, walking	Meticulously clean your Family/Health gua and remove any advertisements for food, or loud synthetic or plastic colors. Fortify this area with hints of green and natural elements of simplicity, such as a plant. The element Earth corresponds to the stomach in Chinese medicine—your relationship area, so clean and embellish your Relationships/Romance gua.

ACTIVITY: DEFINING YOUR INTENTIONS FOR FAMILY AND HEALTH

Use the space provided here to focus on your intentions for family and health.

Write down the names of all your immediate family members. For each family member, list an adjective or two that describes him or her. Have they done anything nice for you lately? If so, list it. Is there anything they have done recently to hurt your feelings? If so, list it. Now list one wish for your relationship with that family member. You can also write the names of deceased family members along with a few lines describing them and describing what you choose to remember most about them.

Names of Family Member	Adjective	Notes

What does it mean to you to be healthy? What habits do you have that are healthy? What habits do you have that are not healthy? What are your goals for your health, such as staying healthy, recovering from illness, or strengthening certain organs that frequently get sick?

_____

_____

_____

_____

_____

_____

_____

_____

_____

_____

Additional Resources

Bringing Up Parents: The Teenager's Handbook by Alex J. Parker, Ph.D., is filled with helpful, amusing tips for teaching your parents how to act like adults.

Stepliving for Teens: Getting Along with Stepparents, Parents, and Siblings by Joel D. Block et al. offers some great tips for family relationships.

The Yellow Emperor's Medicine Classic by Zhou Chuncai is a fun book done in comic-book format that describes Chinese medicine and is a treatise on health and long life.

The Simple Path to Health by Kim Le is a book to teach you healthy eating patterns.

7

Wealth: Wind

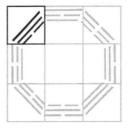

The Wealth area of your room is located in the far left corner from the door, the mouth of chi. This area represents money, prosperity, abundance, your cash flow, and your financial state. This is where you focus to increase your wealth, understand your finances, enjoy affluence, open doors to financial opportunity, and experience luck and fortune.

The Wealth area is symbolized by the forces of the wind. Wealth that comes to us easily can be spent just as easily, as if whisked away in the breeze.

Money and wealth can strongly influence—even control—our lives. If you can learn in your teen years how to take control of your own attitudes regarding wealth, then you will increase your chances of attaining financial security later in life. Most of us learn our attitudes regarding money—everything from how we spend and save to what we think we can or should acquire—from the attitudes of the adults in the households where we grow up. Early experiences with money will also shape our attitudes and expectations. Those born into wealthy families will experience a degree of luxury that will shape their view of the world. Likewise, those born into poverty will experience a degree of scarcity that will shape their view of the world. Some of us may have a tendency to overspend with no regard for consequences, while others may tend to save at the expense of denying the self. Some may tend to spend money on objects, others on experiences.

Despite the influences of your home and family, you can choose how you relate to money. Have you ever really thought about why you treat money the way you do and what you might want to change about it? Magically enough, how you relate to money will tend to determine how money relates to you.

Spend-Nothing Day

A profound way to gain money consciousness is to challenge yourself to spend nothing for one day. Do not allow cash or ATM cards or credit cards to pass through your hands for twenty-four hours. You can decide how strict you want to be—whether or not you count talking on the phone or riding in a car as spending money. Even if your buy-nothing day is simply about not spending any money on the street—making your lunch instead of buying it or spending time reading in a park or library instead of going to a movie—it's amazing to discover how difficult this is. Environmentalists around the world have promoted the concept of organized spend-nothing days to combat wasteful, earth-destroying, overconsumption. Whether or not you share their views regarding the world economy, going one day without spending money is a radical action to assist you in developing an honest awareness of how you handle money and how money handles you.

ACTIVITY: WHERE DID ALL MY MONEY GO?

The first step to develop money consciousness is to become aware of your spending habits. Do you know how much money you spent this week? Can you answer the following questions?

I spent this much money on entertainment: $_____.

The food I ate cost: $_____.

I spent this much money on clothes: $_____.

I earned $_____ for which I paid $_____ in taxes.

The value of the wardrobe I wore this week is $_____.

My Internet connection cost $_____ for the week.

I rang up this amount of charges on my phone bill: $_____.

I traveled in vehicles that used $ _____ worth of gas.

I used _____ gallons of hot water at the cost of $_____ per gallon.

I used_____kilowatts of electricity at the cost of $_____ per kilowatt.

The overall value of the household products that I consumed (toothpaste, toilet paper, napkins, body products, makeup, cleaning supplies, etc.) this week is $_____.

The total weekly cost of rent/mortgage + car insurance + health insurance + house insurance + property taxes + interest payments on loans and credit cards + trash and recycling + lawn care + saving for vacation + dental work + home repairs + charitable contributions and memberships in my household is $_____.

The fact is, whether it's our money or someone else's money, each of us spends a lot on a regular basis. It's up to you to decide how to spend your money and then act on that choice.

What to Put in the Wealth Gua

- **Money:** This is the perfect gua for your piggy bank or its equivalent. Or use a dollar bill as a decorative element. Your Wealth gua is the best place to keep your wallet and is also a great place for checkbooks, bankbooks, and your purse.

- **Red, purple, and gold:** The colors of wealth—red, purple, and gold—are appropriate in this area.

- **Jewelry:** It is considered lucky to put your most valuable items in the Wealth corner. Most jewelry will naturally glisten in the light, adding sparkling chi to charge this gua.

- **Dressers:** Dressers work well in this spot. They have the added bonus of providing a flat surface upon which to place a jewelry box, lucky personal charms, and other special objects. Be sure to organize the contents of the drawers and that the drawers are kept fully shut.

- **Fish:** Fish symbolize prosperity in feng shui, which is why a fish tank is the first thing seen in many Asian restaurants. Add a fish tank or images of fish on a scroll, painting, or poster. Fish = money.

- **Fountains:** A fountain is superb in the Wealth gua but may disturb your sleep. If you really want a fountain in your room and find that its sound keeps you awake, you can unplug it at night.

- **Computer:** A computer is fine in this location, especially if you use it to receive updated financial information or maintain financial records.

> ## What *Not* to Put in the Wealth Gua
>
> - **Mirrors:** Mirrors are not good here. They symbolize that money may come in, but it is reflected right back out (meaning it's spent immediately).
>
> - **Fire objects:** Candles, a fireplace, or a heater are not good here because symbolically they burn money. If you have a fireplace or heater in your Wealth corner, you can counterbalance it by hanging a red banner or other symbols for wealth, such as a photograph of diamonds cut from a magazine.
>
> - **Exercise equipment:** Avoid placing exercise equipment or weights here—unless you desire to work very hard for your money.

Wealth Gua Possibilities

Most of us would like to create prosperity in our lives. To start your successful experience of abundance, you can empower the Wealth gua of your room by adding the objects suggested in the box "What to Put in the Wealth Gua" on the facing page. In addition to attracting prosperity, maybe you have other aims for your relationship with wealth. Check out the following ideas to help you think up creative ways to personalize your Wealth gua.

- **Inspire your sense of abundance through images of generosity.** Small statues of open, giving hands often symbolize charity. You could create a richly decorated red, purple, or gold box with a coin slot in the top, like a piggy bank. A beautiful open bowl to collect coins for an offering to your favorite charity is another wonderful way to remind yourself to help out others when you can.

- **Strive for a simple lifestyle.** Find objects that represent both the simplicity and fertility of nature, such as lush plants, especially the jade plant and bamboo. Healthy, growing plants attract wealth while reminding us that the greatest pleasures often come from the peace of nature. You want your plants to be healthy so make sure to use plants that will do well in your environment. If your room gets a lot of sun, choose flowering plants that like direct sun. If it's dark in your Wealth gua, stick with plants that don't require a lot of light. Bamboo plants will do nicely here and require very little maintenance. Remember not to select spiny plants with sharp thorns or pointed leaves—and feel free to add silk flowers, especially those that are purple or red, when your plant's flowers die back.

- **Attract LOTS of money.** No need to overload your Wealth gua with so much yang that it throws the rest of your room out of balance. Instead, take a moment to focus more clearly on *why* you want lots of money, and then incorporate your answers into your design scheme. For example, if you want the opportunity to shop at all the best stores, one small item representing that luxury will do—a shopping bag from a fancy store, or a particular ad from a magazine cut out and displayed neatly as a poster. You can also use the simple and direct symbol to attract wealth: the dollar bill. Be sure to use a fresh new bill. To increase wealth, you can wrap the bill around a large natural crystal. An amethyst is a good choice because it is purple. Whatever you decide to place, be sure to choose one symbol and display it well without cluttering your Wealth gua. A classic Chinese symbol for wealth is a collection of coins. Many feng shui practitioners recommend using Chinese coins to enhance the Wealth gua. Three coins tied together with red cord can be placed in your Wealth gua to attract fortune. You can also place three tied coins in the Wealth gua on the surface of your desk in order to encourage financial returns on your work.

The Paper Trail of Clutter

Bank notices, school loan information, credit card slips, and check stubs can all take up a lot of space. As a teen, your financial paperwork might be fairly straightforward and limited, but as your financial responsibilities grow, so do your mounds of paperwork. Establishing clutter-free record-keeping habits now will pay off down the line when money managing becomes a fact of life. Here are some basic strategies for keeping the paper trail off your desk and floors.

The more we learn to operate in the world based on trust in our intuition, the stronger our channel will be and the more money we will have.

—SHAKTI GAWAIN

- ☯ **Store financial data electronically.** Financial planning software can also help you organize checkbooks and budgets. More and more, banks, businesses, and credit institutions conduct financial interactions over the Internet. This option may have some security risks, but it certainly can cut down on your paperwork.

- ☯ **Use binders to neatly file records.** You are most likely familiar with the concept of sectioning off a notebook binder by subject for school. You can do the same thing with your financial reports. Keep one binder to neatly store your bank records and another binder for regular incoming bills, such as school loans or credit card bills. Use the colors of wealth—red, purple, and gold—for your binder selections.

- ☯ **Establish one space where you will keep your incoming mail.** Sort through it the day it arrives instead of tossing it on your desk, chair, or the floor. Discard all junk mail right away. Unless you're going to buy from a catalog within the next week, recycle it. If this month's magazine arrives in the mail today, last month's is due for the recycling bin. Reserve one basket or folder for bills to be paid or letters to be answered, and place this basket in a spot where you can easily see it and access it.

☯ **Use your wallet consciously.** Don't let your wallet become full of paper clutter. One source of clutter in the wallet is credit card or ATM receipts, but phone numbers collected from friends, random scraps of papers advertising special events, and other paper goodies can accumulate and create clutter. Keep it simple and reserve your wallet for cash, phone cards, credit cards, identification, and maybe a punch card for movie rentals (ten punches equals one free rental). Your wallet should open easily—without its contents falling out. Broken zippers, overstuffed pockets, or holes are clearly bad chi and will hold you back financially. The money you invest in a decent wallet is worth it. And when you're wallet shopping, remember that red and purple wallets are luckiest. Organize your money by amount, ones, then fives, tens, and so on, with every bill face up.

Bedroom Aquariums

Fish are considered very lucky in feng shui, particularly in the Wealth gua. But some feng shui practitioners do not suggest fish tanks in the bedroom. The noise of electric air filters can disturb sleep. If you wish to have fish in your bedroom, either use a quiet filter or keep fish in a fish bowl—as long as you're willing to clean the bowl regularly. Ask at the pet store for recommendations regarding water-feeding plants for your aquarium or fish bowl. These "floating" plants serve as a natural filter for the water while providing extra life and joy to both your room and your fish. Use the colors of wealth—purple and red—for the marbles or stones and other items in your aquarium or fish bowl. Red fish are the most lucky.

ACTIVITY: WHAT YOU THINK ABOUT MONEY

Use these prompts to think about your attitudes toward money.

I believe money is:_____

_____

_____

I learned about money from:_____

_____

I keep my money in a (circle those that apply): checking account /
    savings account / money market / mutual fund / IRA / trust fund /
    liquid assets such as a car in my name / piggy bank

When I have extra cash, the first thing I buy is:_____

_____

When I'm older, I'd like to have enough money to: _____

_____

_____

_____

I'll want a salary of about: $_____

I touched money _____ times today.

What I'd like to change about my spending and attitude toward
    money is:

_____

_____

_____

Wealth Mouth of Chi

The entryway of your house affects the wealth of your family. If you place your junk near the door as soon as you come in, you may potentially block fortunate opportunities for everyone. While you may not have much say over what others in your household do, you can take care of your own items rather than add to any clutter in the front entrance. Who knows—maybe sloppy siblings or parents will actually follow your lead!

Additional Resources

To learn about finances, start with the money books by Suzie Orman. *Your Money or Your Life* by Suzie Orman describes how the author started out as a waitress in a coffee shop and became a millionare after developing money consciousnesss.

The Motley Fool Investment Guide for Teens by David and Tom Gardner is another popular source for investment tips.

Also check out ***The Tao of Money and Six Simple Principles for Achieving Financial Harmony*** by Ivan Hoffman.

8

Fame/ Reputation: Fire

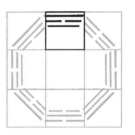

The Fame/Reputation gua of your room is located along the center of the back wall. In feng shui, fame means not only being famous (as in well-known or recognized), but also refers to your reputation, the respect that others have for you, how others perceive you, public attention and acclaim, and popularity. Fame is associated with fire.

Just as light from a single flame can illuminate a dark place, your reputation can reach out to cast your light into a larger area.

Fame means success and public appreciation of your talent. But the concept of reputation takes precedence over the concept of fame on a grand scale. After all, the good opinion of others can inspire your self-esteem, helping you to do well and feel proud of yourself. It is most important, then, to have a good reputation, whether in a community of ten or in a community of ten million.

What to Put in the Fame/Reputation Gua

- **Red, orange, or purple:** Incorporate the colors of fire—red, orange, or purple—into your Fame/Reputation gua, but not to the degree that they are too stimulating and make your room too bright for restful sleep.

- **Fire- and heat-producing objects:** Fire is perfect here, such as candles, fireplaces, or heaters.

- **Electronic equipment:** Computers and electronic equipment are fine here since they produce energy that stimulates this gua.

- **Awards:** Symbols of achievement are good here, such as academic awards or sports trophies.

- **Plants:** Lush plants and colorful flowers are also well placed in this gua.

What *Not* to Place in the Fame/Reputation Gua

- **Water:** This is not a lucky location for watery things such as a fish tank or the colors blue or black. Water extinguishes fire. It can dampen your reputation and diminish your flame.

ACTIVITY: WHAT YOU THINK ABOUT FAME

Complete the following to develop insight into your intentions for the Fame/Reputation gua.

I would describe myself as:_____

_____

_____

_____

My close friends would describe me as:_____

_____

_____

_____

My parents would describe me as:_____

_____

_____

_____

People at school would describe me as:_____

_____

_____

_____

When people first meet me, I want them to see me as: _____

_____

_____

_____

Oh, To Be Famous . . .

It's not surprising that people want to be famous. In the United States, celebrities are like royalty and magazines devoted to them can be found everywhere. Here, fame seems to bring wealth and freedom. The desire for fame is not necessarily a bad thing. We all want to be acknowledged and celebrated for our hard work. The goals of fame, recognition, and accomplishment can be inspiring motivation for achieving things we otherwise wouldn't pursue. The desire for fame becomes unhealthy when you would do *anything* in order to attain it. Most people desire fame for something that is close to their heart—a particular talent or passion. If this is true for you, enhance your Fame/Reputation gua with images of the activities and passions for which you'd like to be famous.

Remember to be your own coach and agent. Famous people have coaches and agents to keep them motivated when they experience a lull. Try placing one meaningful affirmation, such as "I am a strong athlete," or inspirational phrases, such as "Diva-in-training" or "Talent + Perseverance = Attainment," in your Fame/Reputation gua. Pictures of people you admire who are living out your dream also go well in this gua.

Go star sighting—especially when *you* are the star. Fans go out of the way to catch sightings of the famous people they admire. Are you willing to do the same? Are you paying attention to your own accomplishments, no matter how small? Do you defend yourself loyally in the face of opposition? Go out of your way to catch yourself in the act of doing something great, wonderful, and worthy of adoration.

?

Question: *I just found out that my so-called friend Jenna has been spreading lies about me to this guy who likes me because she wants to be with him. Meanwhile, I think I overheard someone in the locker room saying my name and then everyone else laughing, but they all got quiet when I came in the room. I might be paranoid, but it feels like I'm surrounded by a bunch of backstabbers who could care less about me.*

!

Answer: If you're in high school, there's a good chance that you are surrounded by a bunch of backstabbers. People who believe they are unable to make and keep friends based on their own merit frequently try to gain popularity by manipulating social situations and ridiculing others. While you can't make someone become a better person, you can protect yourself from their behavior. Start by ritually fixing your intent through the art of physical placement. Is your bed in the commanding position? Recall that having a wall behind your headboard protects you from surprise attacks. In a similar fashion, good friends will back you up in social situations, so check on your Relationships/Romance gua. Are there items there that should be removed, such as excess clutter? Stabilize your Fame/Reputation corner with some solid, grounded, Earth energy, such as a plant in a clay pot or a wooden sculpture. Embellish your Helpful people/Travel corner too. Make sure to call on stable helpers—older siblings, cool adults, or even books and counselors for support.

Additional Resources

No Body's Perfect: Stories by Teens about Body Image, Sef-Acceptance, and the Search for Identity by Kimberly Kirberger includes short stories, poems, and general words of wisdom from other teens regarding personal identity.

The Scarlet Letter by Nathaniel Hawthorne is the ultimate classic novel for observing the dynamics of reputation.

In Wise-Girl: What I've Learned about Life, Love, and Loss by Jamie-Lynn Singer and Sheryl Berk, The Sopranos star reveals the perks and pressures that accompanied her fame.

9

Relationships/ Romance: Earth

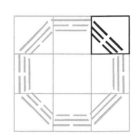

The Relationships/Romance area of your room is located in the far right corner from the entrance. This area represents close friendships and loving partnerships. Here is where you focus to attract new friends, a boyfriend or girlfriend, a significant partner, even a marriage. This area influences your ability to create nurturing relationships, and develop and maintain the quality of those relationships. This is also the corner for romance and love. Just as Earth is the nurturing and regenerative force behind all life, our relationships are what sustain us.

What Goes in the Relationships/Romance Gua

- **Mirrors.** Mirrors go well here, especially in oval or round shapes.

- **All things pink.** The color pink is good here, a color of love.

- **Pictures of loved ones.** This is the perfect place for pictures of your sweetheart or close friends. Just don't place so many friend pictures that a partner can't get in because of all the other people in the way.

- **Paired items.** The Relationships/Romance gua is an ideal place for objects in pairs, such as a pair of candlesticks, two flowers, or two matching crystals. Keep the pairs united.

What *Not* to Put in the Relationships/Romance Gua

- **Television.** A television is not good in this corner because you develop a relationship with TV personalities, not real people, and this leads to too much TV watching.

- **Computers.** A computer is not the best here, unless you plan on meeting a mate online. Otherwise, you will spend too much time on the computer and not enough time relating to others face to face.

What Is a Relationship, Anyway?

You may tend to think of relationships in terms of intimacy with friends, family, or romantic partners. But you are actually in constant relationship with everyone in your immediate environment including people you don't see. For example, if you eat a peach, you have an indirect impact on the farm worker who plucked the peach from its branch. When you are kind to someone, you are also kind to the people who love that person and desire for that person to receive kindness. Our circle of influence is so wide that we truly are all connected.

Relationships can be an incredible resource for growth, a way to explore our own selves, a source of pleasure, company, support, and entertainment. Yet they can also be a source of confusion, frustration, disappointment, and hurt. Just as many of us live in the discomfort of disorganized, out of balance rooms because we've never experienced the benefits of an orderly and balanced space, many of us live in the discomfort of out-of-balance relationships because we haven't learned habits of healthy relating. In feng shui terms, when relationships are in accordance with the natural principles of the universe, our interactions with others bring optimal chi and all involved are blessed. When our relationships are not guided by the universal principles, we experience discomfort and conflict. To establish relationship balance, apply the three basics of feng shui:

☯ **Remove clutter.**

☯ **Unblock the mouth of chi.**

☯ **Proper placement.**

Remove Relationship Clutter

We all spend a lot of time with family, teachers, and peers, regardless of whether we want to or not. Interactions can sometimes be emotionally charged. When we let subtle resentments and hurts build up, it creates emotional clutter. This clutter can confuse us or surface at all the wrong moments. Little innocent statements become grandiose accusations. Your best friend says "Pass the salt, please" and you're hearing "and, on top of everything I've ever asked of you—including borrowing your favorite sweater that, by the way, I've stained—continue to serve me by passing the salt." Before you know it, you are considering throwing the salt shaker at her. Avoid flying salt shakers by not allowing emotional clutter to pile up. If an intimate friend or family member has crossed your personal boundaries, hurt your feelings, or behaved in a way that upset you, take a moment to deal with the conflict at the time. As the *Tao Te Ching* says:

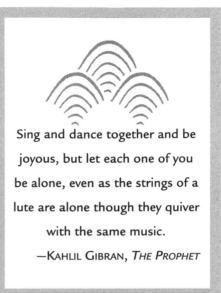

Sing and dance together and be joyous, but let each one of you be alone, even as the strings of a lute are alone though they quiver with the same music.

—KAHLIL GIBRAN, *THE PROPHET*

> *Prevent trouble before it arises.*
> *Put things in order before they exist.*

Relationship Mouth of Chi

What is the mouth of chi in your relationships? It's literally your mouth, your direct line of communication. Chi develops in our relationships through what we express in the form of words, hands, body movements, or facial expression. If the lines of communication are blocked, it will be challenging to create and enjoy healthy and harmonious relationships.

Think of it this way: you can have the fastest, shiniest, best computer in the world, but if your call-waiting bumps you off the internet every single time, your connection isn't working the way it should. In the same sense, you could be the most attractive, confident, talented, unique, and glorious

ACTIVITY: RELATIONSHIP CLUTTER

Write down the names of three close friends.

_____

_____

_____

Now write down the name of either a sibling, parent, or guardian.

_____

Take a moment to think about your relationships with these people. Are there any pieces of emotional clutter in the corners of your mind? Write down anything you can think of that any of these people has done to hurt your feelings or upset you.

_____

_____

_____

_____

_____

_____

Look at the items on your list. Circle the ones that are major upsets. Look at the remaining items on the list. Are they small stuff? Ask yourself if there are any items on the list that you are willing to release. Take your pen or pencil and cross out each item as if you are throwing it away and say to yourself, "I forgive (person's name) for (offending act)." Congratulations. You just cleaned up some relationship clutter.

human being in the world, but if you have a hard time communicating with others, chances are your relationships are going to be incredibly uncomfortable.

Relationship counselors frequently recommend some of the following strategies for maintaining good communication.

Say What You Mean and Mean What You Say

Unblocking communication means daring to be honest and straight-forward with people. This doesn't mean walking up to everyone you know and sharing everything on your mind: "Hey, Sally, I think it's time you try some deodorant. And Andy, those glasses are really ugly." What it does mean is expressing yourself based on your own beliefs and not what you think others will approve. Simply tell your truth.

Use "I" statements

Blocked chi can build pressure that, when released, can be explosive. The use of "I" statements can help you release chi in a balanced manner, instead of exploding with inner frustrations. An "I" statement is a statement where all of the verbs are in the first person. For example, you might want to talk with your best friend who borrows your clothes and returns them in poor condition. Your head might think: "You ALWAYS take my stuff and NEVER give it back on time. What is WRONG with you? Do you think I LIKE walking around with ketchup stains on my favorite, favorite sweater? You are such an inconsiderate _____ (fill in your favorite irresponsible noun)." That is definitely not an "I" statement. It automatically puts the listener on the defensive. Now, what if, instead, you said: "I felt disrespected when you borrowed my sweater, got a stain on it, and didn't give it back to me for six months. I had really wanted to wear it last week because it goes perfectly with my new pants. I interpreted your keeping it for so long as your not caring about my needs. I'm wondering if, should I lend you anything in the future, you could make more of an effort to take better care of my things." Chances are your friend would be more receptive to your comments and might actually change her behavior based on you telling your truth. In reality, most of us have a hard time remembering to use "I" statements when we're angry, but it's a great strategy to be aware of, particularly in times of heated conflict when you really want another person to hear what you have to say.

Listen

Once you've shared your experience, the person you are speaking with may have a few things to say in response. Don't be surprised if that person can't understand your point right away. It's very difficult for people to listen, especially if they feel threatened by what you are saying. Take the time to listen to them thoughtfully and hear what *they* are saying, as well. When people feel heard, they're also more prone to listen. Sometimes it helps to show someone that you are listening and make sure you're hearing them correctly by repeating their statements back to them: "So what I hear you saying is. . . ." Try this on a parent sometime and watch the startled expression on their face as they realize you actually heard what they said!

Protect Yourself

Sometimes no matter how evolved our personal communication skills are, we can still be thrown off balance by the poor communication skills or overwhelming sha chi of others.

- ☯ **Avoid unhealthy relationships.** Most of us can intuitively sense whether or not someone is good for us. When we relate well with someone, we find ourselves able to be whomever we want, express our true feelings, and behave in ways that feel good to us. Less healthy relationships are the ones where we try to change ourselves in order to please others, have to watch what we say or do out of fear of judgment or repercussion, and find ourselves behaving in ways that undermine our sense of personal integrity.

- **Use humor to disintegrate and deflect sha chi like a crystal.** A crystal can take a dark cloud of sha chi and break it into thousands of sparkling little pieces of light (see Feng Shui Cures on pages 181–182 for more information on crystals). In relationships, humor can act like a crystal and can transform tension into laughter.

- **Mirror back the image.** Frequently people are unaware of the degree of sha chi that they are sending out. Sometimes mirroring their own behavior back to them is all it takes to stop poor behavior in its tracks. After years of being bullied by her older brother, a teen finally decided she was no longer going to accept her brother's insults as truth. The next time he called her stupid, she calmly countered, "You just insulted me by saying I was stupid." The brother looked shocked and answered: "No I didn't! You're crazy. Why do you have to be so sensitive?" But she didn't lose ground and continued mirroring: "Now you are calling me crazy and over-sensitive." After a few more interactions along those lines, the brother actually stopped himself mid-insult one day and rephrased the sentence in a totally different way. The mirroring worked.

- **Utilize the controlling element.** Chapter 13 explains how controlling elements can be used to balance a room. In terms of relationships, the controlling element might be a responsible third party who can provide some safety and a possible quick resolution to avoid an escalating conflict. In some cases, bringing in a controlling element is the most direct fix for someone who is unable to respect your boundaries or who threatens your physical safety. Whether it be a teacher, police officer, parent, mediator, or other authority figure, call on controlling elements to intervene in difficult and unsafe social situations.

UNBLOCK YOUR RELATIONSHIPS

Look again at the four names you used for the exercise on page 120 and each item enclosed in a circle. Which of these items represent a blocked mouth of chi in your relationship? Write down everything that you wish to say to that person regarding the conflict. Use as many pieces of paper as you need. Now go back to what you've written and cross out anything that, on reflection, is small stuff. Look back at what is left and begin a new paragraph, converting everything that you've written into an "I" statement. Be willing to unblock your mouth of chi and communicate your "I" statements to your friend, sibling, parent, or guardian.

Relationship Placement

Not everyone is going to be your friend. And not everyone you have a crush on is going to be a relationship partner. We can all simplify our relationships by understanding the role they play in the eight areas of life. For most of us, a parent or guardian, sibling or best friend, is going to be central in the decision making and growth process in our life. So it makes sense to focus a lot of our energy on creating balanced relationships with those special people. Other relationships may not play a major role in our lives.

Knowing where people fit in the eight areas of life can be an incredible asset. For example, a teacher may be useful for your Knowledge gua, but not all teachers are necessarily going to be Helpful people to you. Listening to your intuition to tell you who is assisting you in specific ways will help you tune out those who are undermining your efforts to grow as a person. A friend who borrows money might be a wonderful social outlet but horrible on your finances. Understanding the difference between supporting friends emotionally (Relationships/Romance gua) and supporting them financially (Wealth gua) can help you be clear with yourself about your boundaries and needs.

WHERE ARE YOUR RELATIONSHIPS?

Write down the names of ten people who most frequently appear in your life. Next to their names, write down what gua or guas they fit into.

Do you have at least one name in every gua? If not, write down the type of person or relationship you would like to have supporting the missing gua(s).

Person   Gua

1.
_____

2.
_____

3.
_____

4.
_____

5.
_____

6.
_____

7.
_____

8.
_____

9.
_____

10.
_____

Are any of these people creating sha chi in your life because they're in the wrong gua? If so, make note of what gua you'd prefer to see them in.

Finding Romance

?

Question: I know I should be . . . [choose one that applies to you: doing my homework, practicing my instrument, working on my art project, fundraising for the homeless, applying to colleges, creating the next poetic masterpiece of the new millennium, or even cleaning my room] . . . but I just can't seem to stop obsessing about wanting a relationship! What can I do to let go of constant obsession about romance and just allow love to come to me?

!

Answer: Obsessive thinking about romance can be a sign that an individual doesn't trust his or her ability to attract, receive, or deserve good things in life. If this is true for you, place objects that really nurture yourself in the Relationships/Romance gua: body lotions, inspirational poetry, and images that you consider beautiful. These things are all food for your soul. Take yoga and meditation classes to learn to unravel the knots in the mind. All of that mind chatter actually produces sha chi that blocks the possibility for romance. Look in your Relationships/Romance gua and remove any ticking device such as clocks, watches, or even a computer that beeps on a regular basis. They are causing stress and pressuring you to feel as if you don't have enough time to create partnerships. What you are trying to do in your

Symbols of Love

In China, a pair of ducks is a symbol of love, fidelity, and marriage because ducks mate for life. Another symbol of partnership and marriage is a dragon with a phoenix. A pair of ducks in the form of stuffed animals, posters, or trinkets, or a print or embroidery of a dragon and phoenix are excellent in the Relationships/Romance gua.

YOUR ROMANTIC INTENTIONS

Complete these statements to gain insight into your intentions for your Relationships/Romance gua.

If I were planning a date with someone, we would:

_____

I want my date to share my enthusiasm for:

_____

The person I would take on this date is:

_____

I choose this person because:

_____

If that person were unavailable the next person I would choose is:

_____

I choose this person because:

_____

Just once I wish someone would say to me:

" _____ "

I believe romance is:

_____

I believe true love is:

_____

The qualities that are most important to me in a relationship partner are:

_____

ACTIVITY: ROMANCE COLLAGE

The Relationships/Romance gua is an excellent location for art that inspires your sense of romantic dreaming. With some simple construction paper, glue, and pictures clipped from magazines, you can create a romance collage to hang in this gua:

Search magazines and newspapers that are ready to be recycled and cut out any images that symbolize romance to you. You can use your answers from Your Romantic Intentions (page 127) to help you come up with ideas. If you prefer, you can combine pictures with words cut out from ads or article headings.

Design your collage by placing your selected images on the construction paper and moving them around until you find a suitable design. Be sure to include things in pairs.

Glue the images in place.

Let the glue dry, leaving the collage for 24 hours. For extra strength, place the collage under a heavy book or surface while it dries.

Hang up your new romance collage in your Relationships/ Romance gua.

Relationships/Romance gua is breathe, relax, invite pleasing sensation, and open your heart. As always, remove all clutter. A nice quartz crystal might lend some crystal-clarity to your thoughts. The scents of fresh flowers or an aromatherapy candle will remind you to relax and bring your focus away from the invisible world of wondering and into the physical world of sensing. Just as a comfortable couch will invite a friend to sit and stay, a relaxed and warm Relationships/Romance gua invited souls looking for romance to come into your space.

?

Question: *I'm in love, but my parents and some friends don't approve because they don't want me to date / we're from different backgrounds/ they're jealous. Anything feng shui can do?*

!

Answer: This question is more about your relationships with disapproving others than your romantic interests. Whether or not we like it, there's more to relationships than romance. Definitely nurture the positive elements of your romantic relationship by allowing romantic expression in your Relationships/ Romance gua. Support your other relationships and clear up miscommunication by making sure the items in this gua are well placed and that the gua is clutter free. Do you have pictures of your disapproving family and friends right next to pictures of your special someone? Perhaps you want to give them all a little space from each other. Try moving pictures of family into the Family/Health gua instead. Make sure that your objects are in pairs and not triplets, quadruplets, or, worse, piles of clutter. A nice rounded crystal can help diffuse tension. If friends or family are disapproving of your love due to social prejudice, fortify either your Relationships/ Romance gua or Helpful people/Travel gua with symbols of justice, inspiration, and pride, adding perhaps, a symbol of the open-lotus to invite the opening of minds and hearts to your path.

Additional resources

Love and Sex: Ten Stories of Truth edited by Michael Cart is a collection of ten short stories dealing with teen love and sexuality—from the pains of a blind date to longing for a first love.

Changing Bodies, Changing Lives: A Book for Teens on Sex and Relationships by Ruth Bell Alexander is an all-inclusive guide to relationships and sexuality based on quotes and stories from hundreds of teenagers.

Go Ask Alice Book of Answers: A Guide to Good Physical, Sexual, and Emotional Health by Columbia University's Health Education Program is a no-holds-barred, comprehensive resource for sex, relationships, and life in general. Or check out the Web site www.goaskalice.com.

10

Creativity/
Children: Lake

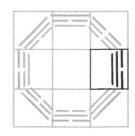

The Creativity/Children gua of your room is located in the center of the wall to your right when you enter from the mouth of chi. This area represents your personal artistic creative expression. It also represents children because creativity is so close to the procreative forces of nature. This gua is associated with the energy of the lake—a peaceful calm that is the optimal environment for creation and where children can safely play. Development of this gua encourages you to freely express and share your creativity. It also helps you relate well to younger children.

A close examination of this gua can assist you in letting go of your identity as a child so you can embrace your new identity as a teen. To encourage your personal growth, remove all childlike possessions, such as stuffed animals or dolls from this gua. If you are a teen parent, this is a wonderful gua in which to place your child or your child's belongings. If you share a room with a much younger sibling, place their bed in this gua.

The Creativity/Children gua is where you focus energy to enhance or motivate your creative process. Use this area for special projects and items that inspire your sense of creativity. How do you define creativity? If you ask most people to define creativity, they usually mention writing poems, painting, or playing a musical instrument. These are wonderful examples of creativity, but it comes in many forms. Even if you don't consider yourself a creative person, chances are you participate in creative projects every day. Creative activities can be as diverse as cooking, sports, making your own clothes, playing with a chemistry set, gardening, computer programming, discovering new shades of makeup and hairstyles, dancing, rapping, or making jewelry.

> What is man's will and how shall he use it? Let him put forth its power to uncover the Atman [the light within], not hide the Atman.
>
> —SWAMI PRABHAVANANDO, FROM THE *SONG OF GOD: BHAGAVAD-GITA*

Creativity offers an outlet for energy that is otherwise not expressed in our lives. That energy may have originally felt like anger, ecstasy, restlessness, or any kind of emotion. Once it becomes creativity, it takes on a life of its own. But opening yourself up to creativity can be a challenging process. Two of the most common offenders for blocking creativity are lack of time and lack of confidence.

Give Yourself Creative Time

To help your creative chi to flow, give yourself time for creative expression. Often creative time is special, undefined time, time that does not necessarily have a defined goal or desired outcome. It can be challenging to give space for this kind of creative time when faced with school, sports, clubs, social engagements, family obligations, and other responsibilities. Other people, particularly those who have suppressed their own creativity, may challenge your choice to retreat from the busy result-oriented world of "producing" into the magical process-oriented space of "creating." Give

Every blade of grass has its Angel
that bends over it
and whispers, "Grow, grow."

—THE TALMUD

yourself the time you need to be creative. For some this may mean committing to one hour every day of a certain activity. For others, it may be setting aside larger blocks of time once or twice a week. Only you know what your creative soul needs.

Trust Your Abilities

Our own lack of confidence can be a major block to accessing creativity. Thoughts that say we're not good enough, not creative enough, or not talented enough will inhibit our actions. Don't let negative thoughts block your creativity. Refuse to give them any real power. Thoughts need not be anything more than passing clouds—things that float by and that you may observe. If the thought is negative, one can simply look at it and watch it float away. After all, it's just a thought. The fact that a thought exists does not make it true.

Creative Object Placement

Creativity means freedom. But it also means the presence of creative tools such as paintbrushes, glue, scrap materials, and multicolored pens. Don't allow these items to overtake your room and become the primary evidence of your creativity. Stash your art tools, music supplies, and other items in organized containers or toolboxes. In this way, you can keep the focus of your room on the real art: your posters, your paintings, your collections, and any finished creative projects you wish to highlight. Regularly storing your tools in a predictable spot also gives you the freedom of knowing where things are when you want them. Identify your creative passion and apply it to organizing your stuff. Take advantage of that pile of old guitars in your room by decorating each one with wild colors or stickers. Make a creative display so that the presence of your instruments supports your

TURNING THE NEGATIVE INTO THE POSITIVE

One incredibly powerful exercise is to write down your negative thoughts as you become aware of them. Next to the thought, write what that thought would look like if it was turned into an affirmative statement. For example, "I'm never going to be good at this. I might as well give it up" becomes "I'm brand new at this and it's going to take some time, patience, and practice before I feel like I can do it well." Write down three negative thoughts that are in your head and, across from them, their positive spin.

Negative Thought   Positive Spin

1._____   _____

_____   _____

_____   _____

_____   _____

2._____   _____

_____   _____

_____   _____

_____   _____

3._____   _____

_____   _____

_____   _____

_____   _____

Inspiration may be a form of superconsciousness, or perhaps subconsciousness—I wouldn't know. But I am sure it is the antithesis of self-consciousness.
—AARON COPLAND, COMPOSER

Creativity/Children gua while remaining both decorative and functional. Cover a portion of your wall with heavy paper and use that as an ongoing canvas for poetry, doodling, or composing. Keep the art within the boundaries of the paper, and keep the paper neatly hung in a position of honor so that it doesn't turn into just another piece of clutter.

Tattoos and Piercings

Creativity is about self-expression. A lot of people explore personal creativity through clothes, hair, piercings, and tattoos. Tattoos are a very ancient form of body art and beautification. Just like any other aspect of feng shui, whenever you make a change, you attract or deflect certain energies. It is best to do so consciously and with clear intentions. If you are thinking of getting a tattoo, consider that you may feel differently about this tattoo as you grow and change. Before choosing your design, ask yourself what image you wish to carry with you your entire life and what energies you wish it to attract. How will those energies move through life with you?

Piercing, beyond being decorative, has very specific physical effects. When you pierce an area of your body, you stimulate a specific acupuncture point. For example, piercing one's ears stimulates eyesight, and piercing this part of the body was popularized by sailors who benefited from seeing land at far distances.

Piercing your eyebrows? Depending on where you pierce it, that's a point on the bladder, stomach, or small intestine meridian. Piercing your chin under your lip? That's a point on your conception vessel that could affect your hormones. Piercing your tongue? Different locations on the tongue stimulate different points. The center of your tongue stimulates a digestion point. In Chinese medicine, nipples are an area that is not

What to Put in the Creativity/Children Gua

This is the gua for items of personal creative expression.

- **Art supplies:** If you are an artist place your easel or art supplies here, if a writer your desk, and if a musician your musical instruments or recording equipment.

- **Artwork:** All beautiful embellishments are superb here, especially things that are fun and artistic. This is the perfect place for posters and art that you love or that you created.

- **White:** The color white is the color of the Creativity/ Children gua. White flowers, such as orchids work well here.

- **Computer:** A computer can also inspire new ideas and be a tool for creating art, be it visual art or creative writing.

What *Not* to Put in the Creativity/Children Gua

- **TV:** Viewing TV can give you creative ideas but can drain your creative energy if you watch it too frequently, simply observing the creativity of others and not developing your own. If you place a TV in this gua, keep it tucked neatly into a cabinet that can be closed so it doesn't always dominate your view. If you don't have a cabinet, simply hang a piece of fabric over the screen when it is off to cover the glare from the screen.

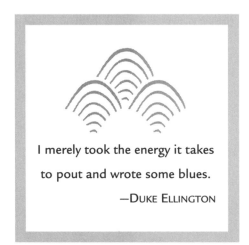

I merely took the energy it takes to pout and wrote some blues.
—DUKE ELLINGTON

pierced. A ring in the navel for too long can deplete your immune system. If you want to know what points will be activated by a piercing, go to an acupuncturist and get a diagnosis. Then you can plan piercings to help you sustain good health.

Additional Resources

The Artists Way by Julia Cameron offers a twelve-week program to develop your inner artist.

www.poetryslam.com is a great Web site introduction to the art of performance poetry. The site includes a map of poetry slam listings across the United States.

www.teenink.com is the Web site of *Teen Ink,* a Web zine and book series written by teens for teens. Review the poetry, art, and photography of others or submit your own.

11

Helpful People/
Travel: Heaven

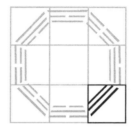

The Helpful people/Travel gua is located in the nearest right corner when you enter your room. The Helpful people/Travel gua represents those who help you, guide you, and offer wisdom and advice in your life. This gua is associated with heaven, as if helpers were sent from heaven like angels. It is also associated with travel.

According to the Tao, all things are interdependent. As you help others, others help you. Help can mean financial assistance to meet someone's needs, physical help to complete a task, emotional help, or spiritual guidance. Helpers can be friends, family members, teachers, counselors, patron saints, pets, and mystical beings. Sometimes the most significant helpers come in the form of strangers who happen to say just the right things at just the right time. Most of us tend to take for granted the helpful people in our lives. This is all the more reason to be mindful of what is in this corner. Clutter in this area will block your chances to meet the right

137

I get by with a little help from my friends.

—THE BEATLES

people, network, make contacts, and go places. Give this area special attention if you deeply need the assistance and good favor of others, such as when you are applying to colleges or feel alone in the middle of conflicts at school, at home, or with friends.

In my feng shui practice I notice that the Helpful people/Travel gua is neglected. Clients are more interested in the Wealth gua or the Relationships/Romance gua. But it was the healing of the Helpful people/Travel gua that transformed the writing career of my friend Donna. Donna was a successful writer who had received huge financial rewards and extensive public attention for her novel. Due to her success, she moved to a larger apartment. Within a short while of moving into her new place she noticed a drop in her press coverage and began feeling increasingly lonely.

What to Put in the Helpful People/Travel Gua

- **Pictures of your helpers:** Use the wall space in this area for pictures and images of saints, spirits, angels, or personal heroes.

- **Tools for networking:** This is a great place for a phone or Internet connection. A computer in this area can help with networking opportunities as well as locating help hotlines or opportunities for travel.

- **Travel-related objects:** A poster of a place you would like to visit works nicely in this gua, as does a map of the world or a globe.

- **Television:** A TV goes nicely in this gua because television programs connect us to the external world.

Discovering Helpers

Potential helpers can come in many forms. Identify people who fit in the following categories to discover your potential helpers:

Teachers

Counselors

Friends

Friendly acquaintances

Networks from clubs, school, sports, associations

Hotlines

Coaches

Mentors

Supervisors

Spiritual teachers

Wise elders

Books

Siblings

Relatives: aunts, uncles, cousins, grandparents, godparents

Animals

Spirit guides

Police

Firefighters

Political leaders

Friendly community members

Your own intuition

Roadside towing assistance

Medical professionals

Alternative health practitioners (masseurs, acupuncturists, etc.)

Seeking an answer, Donna asked me to feng shui her studio apartment. Unintentionally, Donna had done a pretty good job with her Career and Wealth guas. But her Helpful people/Travel gua was completely neglected. A large storage closet was located in this gua. It was so full that the door could not close. The closet was filled with boxes. They spilled over into the Career gua entrance, blocking the mouth of chi to her front door, as well. I had to slide between boxes to enter the room. Donna was so overwhelmed by her boxes of junk that she didn't want to sort through them. With my assistance, she went through the boxes and donated almost all of the contents. Donna organized the closet and was able to open the door to her house without stumbling over boxes. She bought new padded hangers for her clothes and new storage boxes for her winter sweaters. She hung a decorative oval mirror on the outside of the closet door at eye level in order to expand the space and attract light to that gua.

Within a month of cleaning out the closet, Donna was contacted by a well-known San Francisco magazine and asked to be featured in one of their articles. In addition, a travel opportunity that Donna had not foreseen came to pass (remember that this is also the gua of Travel). Donna was invited to go to Germany for a series of book signings. Her trip resulted in book contracts for two more novels! Donna and I gloated over the success of feng shui and the instant result of cleaning out her closet.

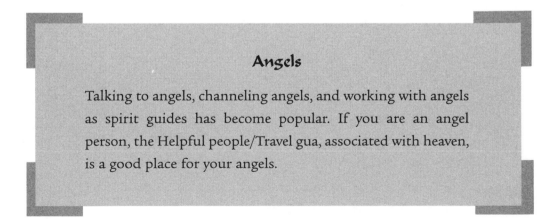

Angels

Talking to angels, channeling angels, and working with angels as spirit guides has become popular. If you are an angel person, the Helpful people/Travel gua, associated with heaven, is a good place for your angels.

DEFINING YOUR INTENTIONS FOR YOUR
HELPFUL PEOPLE/TRAVEL GUA

Use the following space to make a few notes about the helpful people
in your life. Have you ever asked for help? What happened? Who
would you go to now if you needed help?

_____

_____

_____

_____

_____

Use the space below to make notes on your intentions for travel in
your life. If you could travel anywhere in the world, where would you
like to go and why?

_____

_____

_____

_____

Choosing Helpful People Wisely

A tricky path to maneuver can be that of discerning who is helping and who may be hurting. Sometimes even the best of intentions can mislead. And sometimes people who offer help don't have the best intentions. A good tip to remember, when assessing whether or not someone is a true helper, is that accepting someone's help doesn't mean relinquishing personal power. It is empowering yourself to take the initiative to find someone with the resources you need to accomplish a task or a goal. It is also empowering yourself with the receptivity to accept the support of the universe. Chances are, if another person is asking you to give up personal power (in the form of blind acceptance of a truth or not participating in decision making, for example) they are not actually serving as helpful people. This doesn't mean that we necessarily like all of our helpers. Sometimes a helper can be someone who points out a truth to us and, in order to avoid hearing that truth we end up resenting our helper. It's preferable, however, to have helpful people that simultaneously inspire, assist, and are fun to be around. If you find yourself in a place where you can't name one helper who meets any of these qualities it may be an indication that you are not in the supportive environment that embraces your destiny. Now may be the perfect time to network with new social groups.

Additional Resources

Teens with the Courage to Give: Young People Who Triumphed Over Tragedy and Volunteered to Make a Difference by Jackie Waldman shared the stories of 30 teens who surmounted difficulties in their own lives and become helpful people to others.

12

Career: Water

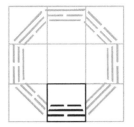

The Career area of your room is located in the center of the wall nearest where you enter your room. This gua represents what you do for a living, your vocation, and how you contribute to society through the work you do. Here is where you focus to create a career and to understand what you want to do for a living. The career gua is associated with the energy of water. Just as water flows along the banks of a river, your career is a journey that shifts as you move through life.

We've all heard the question, "What do you want to be when you grow up?" This is the gua to embellish in order to help you answer that question. Perhaps you're uncertain what career—or careers—you want to pursue. Or perhaps you already know exactly the sort of work you want to do and your school classes and college applications are lined up perfectly to support your goals. Regardless of your certainty or lack thereof concerning your future career, the Career gua is worth paying attention to.

If you need a job now, concentrate on this area, making it free of clutter. If a door is located here, make sure it can open completely and that nothing is kept behind it—you don't want to block your opportunities.

> If you follow your bliss, you put yourself on a kind of track, which has been there all the while waiting for you, and the life that you ought to be living is the one you are living.
>
> —Joseph Campbell

Finding Your Career Path

Career can become an incredibly stressful pressure looming over our head—particularly when we haven't yet started one. Parents may have one plan in mind for us while we may have another. Those who know what they want to do at an early age are often criticized by others for not taking more time to "find themselves," while those who dabble in many things and are willing to admit they don't know what they want are criticized for being "slackers." Early focus on a career will allow you to build a high level of skill in a particular area where dabbling in many things will provide a certain insight and flexibility gained by the generalist. Life usually provides the timelines we need to make decisions as well as the criteria we need along the way. One of the best ways to relieve the stress of deciding a career is to stop asking "Who do I want to be?" in terms of career (that question belongs more in the Knowledge gua) and think more about "What do I want to do, and what do I need to do it?"

What Counts As a Career?

Your Career gua can apply to anything from supporting your school

Tip: Find ways to reinforce your dreams with images of your desired goal.

What to Put in the Career Gua

- **Water-related items:** Career is the water gua, so all things water related are supportive, as are metals, which nurture water.

- **Mirrors:** If you have space in this area, a clean mirror is perfect. Mirrors represent water in feng shui.

- **Books:** Books on subjects that you're interested in as potential career paths go well here.

- **Computers:** Your computer goes well here because you can use it for research, preparing résumés and applications, and networking.

- **Images to support your career goals:** If you are focused on applying for colleges, this is a wonderful spot to place school banners, achievements awards, and posters of the school you wish to attend. If you plan to be a marine biologist, place an image of the undersea world in this gua. If you plan to be a DJ place your mixing equipment or the logo of your favorite radio station here.

activities to promoting job opportunities. What determines this is your intent as an individual. Is your primary focus getting into a good college so that you might have more job options as a professional down the line? Do you need to focus more on having work that supports your immediate living needs? The answers to these questions will help you set up your Career gua in a way that supports your unique needs.

A common assumption is that we work only to make money—money to have a house, money to buy food, and money to raise children. If we

WHAT YOU ENJOY = A CAREER

Often the seeds of what you will do for your career are reflected in your current interests. What types of things do you like to do? Do you know anyone who gets paid for doing those things? What kind of credentials or training did they acquire to get paid to do those things?

_____

_____

_____

_____

_____

_____

make enough money, we can pay for our children to go to college so that they can learn the skills they need in order to make more money. But according to the Taoists, there's more to work than making money, which is why career has a gua of its own, rather than being part of the Wealth gua.

It's true that in our society work provides the comforts that money can buy. Work can help us feel more secure in a world where everything costs a certain amount. But work is also where we spend most of our time (many of us end up spending more time with coworkers than with our own families), where we interact with other people, and, ideally, where we use our talents and creativity to contribute to society. When work does not satisfy us on a personal level, it begins to feel oppressive. So it makes sense to use the opportunities we have to direct our working lives into activities and environments that we enjoy and that help us grow.

Identifying Work That Works for You

Most likely your school has a career counselor or a guidance center. Many of these centers have resources to assist you in learning more about different careers and apply to schools that can help you acquire the tools you need to perform particular types of work. They can also assist you with finding internships and entry-level jobs in your field of interest, and even help you to set up informational interviews with people who are working in different careers. Embellish both your Career gua and Helpful people/Travel gua before you meet with a career counselor.

Whether or not you are ready to think about it, your career path is taking shape around you. The choices you make today open up new opportunities, shape your perspectives, and can broaden or limit your future choices. Some of your friends might be college bound and others might be discovering new talents in vocational or internship programs. Do you know where you are in relation to your career?

Say my friend Joey told me, "As far as I can tell, the only things I like to do are hang out with my friends and play video games. Work's a total hassle. Maybe I'm just not ready to think about career."

Timing is important, and it sounds like Joey's clearly not feeling an urgency to hop on a career path. That's great news, because that gives him lots of time to explore options that will be more exciting to him! Work is always going to be a hassle if you are doing something that bores you, so the goal is for Joey to find work that excites him. At the moment, he's clearly drawing a blank when it comes to options. But he did give us some

The worker feels himself only when he is not working; when he is working he does not feel himself. He is at home when he is not working, and not at home when he is working. His labour is forced labour. It is therefore not the satisfaction of a need but a mere means to satisfy needs outside itself . . . it belongs not to him but to another.

—KARL MARX, FROM *ECONOMIC AND PHILOSOPHICAL MANUSCRIPTS*

IDENTIFYING YOUR CAREER GOALS

Use the following prompts to help you think about what type of work you might like to do.

What kinds of jobs have you had, if any?

_____

_____

What do you currently seek in a job?

_____

_____

What type of job do you think you would enjoy doing for a long time?

_____

_____

What are your current skills?

_____

_____

What are skills that you would like to learn?

_____

_____

What would you like to get paid to do?

_____

_____

clues when he said "the only things I like to do are hang out with my friends and play video games." So let's start there. Chances are, Joey's going to enjoy work that allows him to be social and meet people who interest him. So, pretend you're Joey and take a moment and write down the names of the people who interest you and the qualities that interest you the most. Now, next to each quality, write one kind of job that you can think of where someone with that particular quality might want to work. Now you've come up with some options. Let's move on to video games for a moment. Shall we imagine what it is that Joey likes about video games? The graphics? The competition? The opportunity to get better and better at something? The opportunity to tune out the rest of the world for a while and loose

Strategies for Finding Your Career Path

- Identify your primary interests

- Identify jobs that engage these interests

- Research the qualifications that are necessary in order to get those jobs

- Talk to people in those professions to find out more about what they do during the course of a typical day

- Look for "entry-level" positions with businesses or organizations that are involved with the type of work you are exploring

- Create a résumé

- Apply for internships

- Take classes in your areas of interest

yourself and your mind in concentration? Depending on your answer, you can come up with lots of paths for Joey to research: Someone who loves graphics may actually want to research what it takes to become a video game designer. Someone who plays in order to compete might like a risk-taking business environment. Someone who likes to have something to focus on might enjoy a problem-solving computer position, such as an architectural draftsperson. You can use your current interests as a launching pad for exploring career options, no matter what your interests are. It's just a matter of asking the right questions: What do I like about that thing? What jobs exist that have the quality that I like? Of all of the things I'm interested in, what jobs most possess the qualities that I like?

Additional Resources

Crossing the Unknown Sea: Work as a Pilgrimage of Identity by David Whyte combines personal stories and poems to explore the significance of work in one's life.

Letters to a Young Poet by Rainer Maria Rilke shares the correspondence between a well-known Austrian poet and an aspiring artist.

What Color Is My Parachute by Richard Nelson Bolles is a classic resource for anyone seeking to identify a career path.

Part 4

Elements, Astrology, Feng Shui Cures, and Beyond

By now you've taken the major steps of clearing out your clutter, unblocking the mouth of chi, placing the large items in your room, assessing the eight areas of your life, and adjusting each gua in your room. It's time to observe how the individual guas are interacting with one another. Before proceeding any further, check in with the current state of your room. Go back to the exercise on page 20 and try it again. How's your chi checking out? Have you kept your mouth of chi unblocked after placing your furniture and belongings in their appropriate guas? If you are satisfied with your answers then you are ready to take your feng shui awareness to another level.

In addition to focusing on proper placement for your stuff, it is essential to balance the flow of chi between each gua—between all the areas of life. For example, if you want to attract a romantic relationship you can enhance the Relationships/Romance gua. But since you can create a good relationship with another only if you have knowledge of yourself, it is also important to develop the Knowledge gua. If you only transform your Wealth gua so that you rapidly gain wealth but neglect other important areas such as Creativity/Children or Family/Health, all your money will not be rewarding.

In the next few chapters we'll expand on the basics of feng shui to explore how elemental energy and astrology can impact the balance in your room. You'll also find cures for common feng shui problems. These tools will help you achieve the strongest degree of balance between the guas of your room to create change in your life.

13

The Five Elements of Feng Shui

Chi manifests as either yin or yang energy. Chi also embodies characteristics known as the five powers, five phases, five virtues, or five elements: Fire, Earth, Metal, Water, and Wood. Although they are called elements, they are not really substances. The five elements are five different types of energy that are constantly moving and interacting with each other.

You can create more harmonious rooms by balancing the five elements to strengthen or reduce any element that seems out of balance. The five elements also enable us to enhance desirable aspects of our personalities and soften less desirable aspects by fine-tuning what we put where in our rooms. Learning about the elements gives you a way to understand and directly influence your relationship with your environment. The elements also offer a wonderful solution to create more balance in your room if you feel limited with proper placement of large objects because of your room's shape or size.

153

Balancing: The Three Cycles

The ancient feng shui masters studied the universe and discovered that each element impacts the others in three different cycles: nurturing, controlling, or reducing. One way the elements interact is through a nurturing cycle. Fire nurtures Earth, because after fire burns, it becomes ash, creating more earth crust. Earth nurtures Metal because metal ores are mined from deep within the earth. Metal nurtures Water because water is contained and carried in metal vessels. Water nurtures Wood because watering trees helps them to grow. Wood nurtures Fire because adding logs to a fire helps it to burn.

Another way in which the elements interact is through the controlling cycle. Fire controls Metal by melting it; Metal controls Wood by cutting it; the roots of trees penetrate the earth to destroy it; Earth controls the flow of water with dikes and dams; and Water extinguishes Fire.

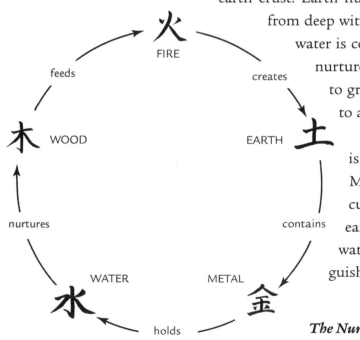

The Nurturing Cycle

The third form of elemental interaction is the reducing cycle. Fire burns Wood; tree roots absorb water; Water corrodes Metal; Metal is extracted from Earth; and Earth suffocates Fire.

The elements are in balance when all five elements are present and no one element excessively dominates.

When assessing the flow of chi in a room, it's important to look at how the different elements interact with each other. If you intuitively "feel" like your room is out of balance but can't quite figure out why, check to see if one (or two) elements are dominating the room. If it is, you can use the controlling or reducing cycles to minimize the impact of that element while applying the nurturing cycle to enhance the other elements.

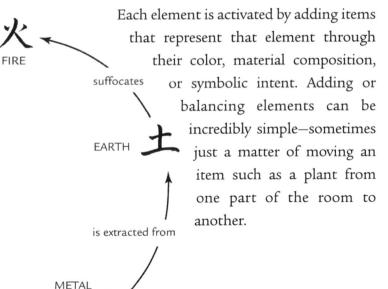

The Controlling Cycle

Each element is activated by adding items that represent that element through their color, material composition, or symbolic intent. Adding or balancing elements can be incredibly simple—sometimes just a matter of moving an item such as a plant from one part of the room to another.

The Reducing Cycle

Colors of the Elements

Black = Water

Gray = Water

Yellow = Earth

Gold = Earth

Green = Wood

Blue = Wood

Orange = Fire

Purple = Fire

Red = Fire

Silver = Metal

White = Metal

Shapes and the Elements

Round/Arch = Metal

Square/Rectangle = Earth

Pyramid/Triangle = Fire

Column/Tall and Thin = Wood

Wavy/Irregular/Curved = Water

Materials and the Elements

Wood Furniture/
  Products = Wood

Paper = Wood

Wicker/Bamboo = Wood

Natural Fibers (Cotton/Hemp/
  Linen) = Wood

Clothes/Shoes = Earth

Bricks/Clay/Soil = Earth

Porcelain/Ceramics = Earth

Heat = Fire

Lights/Sunlight = Fire

Animal Products (Leather/
  Feathers) = Fire

Fire Objects (Candles/
  Stoves) = Fire

Metals (Steel/Brass/
  Silver) = Metal

Hard Stones (Marble/
  Granite) = Metal

Soft Stone (Terra-cotta Tiles/
  Chalk) = Earth

Plaster = Earth

Mirrors = Water

Glass = Water

Aquariums/Fountains = Water

ELEMENTAL ASSESSMENT

What elements are in each of the eight guas of your room?

Gua   **Elements**

Knowledge

Family/Health

Wealth

Fame/Reputation

Relationships/Romance

Creativity

Helpful people/Travel

Career

Once you've filled out the list above, take a moment to answer the following questions:

What elements are most present in your room?

Where do you see the controlling cycle in action?

Where do you see the reducing cycle in action?

Where do you see the nurturing cycle in action?

Enhancing Elements to Suit Your Personality Type

Since the five elements are also part of our individual characters and body composition, you can enhance your room by activating the element or elements that support your body type and disposition. You can also use the three cycles to control elements that might reduce your personal element or to nurture your element. Read the following pages to learn how to find your personal element and discover what things represent each element.

Each element is activated by adding an item or many items that represent that element through their color, material composition, or symbolic intent.

Find Your Element

Each one of us has all five elements in our physical makeup. One or two elements are more dominant than the others. Your dominant element influences many parts of your life—from your health to your way of interacting with the world. There are many ways to determine your dominant element. The easiest and more accurate way is a Chinese pulse diagnosis done by an acupuncturist or doctor of traditional Chinese medicine. Chinese astrology also determines your element. But if you don't have the resources to go to a doctor of Chinese medicine or can't get a professional reading of your Chinese astrology, you can use your intuition to get a better sense of your strong elemental influences. In his book *Feng Shui for Life*, Jon Sandifer offers the following quiz to help you figure out what element you might be and how the elements might be impacting you.

THE ELEMENT QUIZ

Note if any of the statements below relating to the five elements ring true with you. If you feel strongly that you can relate to the statement, then give the appropriate response. Work your way through the various sections. At the end of the exercise, note down which element is emphasized the most.

FACIAL DIAGNOSIS

The fascinating art of facial diagnosis can reveal much about your constitution, drawn from your parents and ancestors. Your bone structure and facial features are unchanging and, like your constitution, represent both your current nature and potential. This section concentrates on physical condition, which changes day by day and week by week. Using a large mirror in a well-lit environment, take a glance at your face. Try not to stare too hard for detail. Discoloration, puffiness, spots, or prominent veins are all related to your current condition. The five primary areas of the face used for diagnosis are shown below.

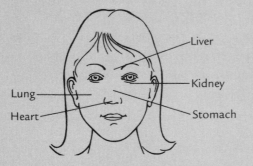

Water: Kidneys

Kidney stagnation is indicated in the area just below your eyes. Look out for signs of puffiness, redness, swelling, or dark bags under your eyes. If these signs appear, you Water element may be out of balance.

Wood: Liver (Gallbladder)

Look in the area above the bridge of the nose, between the eyebrows. Check this area for inflammation, discoloration, spots, dry skin, or deep lines in this area. These signs indicate a weak Wood element.

Fire: Heart

Diagnostically, the heart is represented at the tip of the nose. Does this area appear either swollen, puffy, red, or purple in comparison with the rest of your face? Is it white and pinched like a knuckle on a clenched fist? If this is the case, you may have a weak Fire element.

Earth: Stomach (Spleen/Pancreas)

The stomach is centrally located in the body and is represented in the center of your face—the bridge of your nose. Check this area for redness, yellow tinges, broken capillaries, or a pinched and white appearance like a knuckle on a clenched fist. These signs indicate a weak Earth element.

Metal: Lungs

The lungs are represented throughout the cheek area from below the cheekbone to a line between the corner of the mouth and the edge of the jaw. Check the area for redness, puffiness, broken capillaries, spots, or pale, drawn, grayish skin. These signs demonstrate a weak Metal element.

HABITS

Habits are expressions of your current way of being in the world. See if any of these five areas really strike a chord with you at present. Your "Yes" answers will indicate presence of that element in your composition.

Water

Are you currently less adventurous than usual? Are you being overly cautious or self-protective? Do you find yourself procrastinating and putting off making commitments?

Yes   No

Wood

Have others around you recently criticized you for being insensitive? Are you really listening and aware of the needs of others? Are you being overbearing and domineering? Are you doing everything in a rush?

Yes   No

Fire

Does your life currently seem to be out of control? Are you dashing around in several directions at once, spinning wheels while apparently achieving little? Have others around you recently accused you of being self-centered? Are you erratic in your lifestyle—all action one moment and stillness the next?

Yes   No

Earth

Are you becoming more dependent on others? Do you feel completely overburdened and that your situation is hopeless? Do you have a list of unfinished projects, jobs, letters, conversations? Is there a current tendency in your life to leave things unfinished?

Yes   No

Metal

Are you becoming increasingly isolated in your life? Do you find it difficult to trust those around you? Are you becoming indecisive? Have you noticed that you have become more introverted lately? Are you indifferent to the world outside of yourself?

Yes   No

Cravings can be a normal function that remind us to take in tastes, flavors, and sensations that can support elemental balance. If any of the more extreme attributes listed below ring true, then it can show an imbalance. Try to notice what you are currently drawn to or those things from which you are repelled. In this section your "Yes" answers will reflect a leaning toward that particular element. If you feel your cravings are imbalanced, you may want to nurture that particular element.

Water

Are you attracted to a lot of liquid at present?
Yes   No

Do you prefer your food cold?
Yes   No

Do you add extra salt or soy sauce to your meal? Do you absolutely dislike salt and never use any, even in your cooking?
Yes, I crave salt   No, I hate salt

Wood

Do you currently crave food of a spicy nature? In particular, are you drawn to curry, Thai, or spicy Indian cooking? Do you crave sharp-tasting pickles, lemon, or vinegar? Do you absolutely detest any or all of the above?
Yes, I crave spicy food   No, I hate spicy food

Fire

Are you drawn toward bitter-tasting food? Black coffee? Chocolate? Burnt toast? Do you dislike bitter-tasting greens like kale, spring greens, or chard?
Yes, I crave bitter food   No, I dislike bitter food

Earth

Are you currently craving sweet, creamy, comforting foods? Are you attracted to sweet-tasting dairy products? Do you have a sweet tooth? Are your cravings self-indulgent?

Yes, I crave sweet food   No, I hate sweet food

Metal

Are you drawn toward dry foods—cookies, toast, crackers? Do you prefer your food to be very well cooked—roasts, bakes, and casseroles? Are you drawn toward strong condiments such as pepper, mustard, or horseradish? Do you have occasional cravings for strong, spicy food like a curry?

Yes, I strongly crave these foods   No, I hate these foods

TIME OF DAY

In Chinese medicine, the five major organs and their complementary elements have a particular time of day when they recharge and revitalize. It can be very revealing if you consistently feel a certain way at a particular time of the day. In this section, a "Yes" answer may indicate the need to nurture that element.

Water: Midnight–6 A.M.

Are you restless between these hours? Do you have difficulty sleeping? Are you a night person?

Yes   No

Wood: 6–10 A.M.

Are you at your worst in the morning? Do you dislike having to get up? Do you not begin to function until after 10 A.M.? Do you always wake up early and are unable to go back to sleep?

Yes   No

Fire: 10 A.M.–2 P.M.

Do you have low energy at this time? Do you feel overburdened or uninspired between these hours? Do you lack the enthusiasm that others around you may have at this time of day? Do symptoms generally recur between these hours?

Yes   No

Earth: 2–6 P.M.

Do you lose your inspiration at this time of day? Do you feel tired? Do you need a nap? Do you want to lift your energy with something sweet? Do general symptoms persistently recur during these hours?

Yes   No

Metal: 6 P.M.–midnight

Is this your worst time of day? Do you feel withdrawn, isolated, and antisocial at this time? Are you always tired between these hours? Do you always eat late—close to midnight?

Yes   No

PHYSICAL EXPRESSION

It is a lot easier to read body language in others. But with a little practice, it is easy to notice how you are sitting, how you walk, and how you express yourself physically—even in conversation. "Yes" answers in this section indicate a strong presence of the corresponding element.

Water

Are you overly protective in your body language? Do you have a tendency to cross your legs? Do you fold your arms across your lower belly? Do you want to sit in the commanding position to "protect" yourself when in a room by positioning your back near the wall or positioning yourself so that you can always see the door?

Yes   No

Wood

Do you always walk fast? Is there a certain stiffness to your gait? Are your movements jerky? Do you tend to clench your teeth or jaw?

Yes   No

Fire

Are you very animated in your expression? Do you constantly gesticulate with your hands and arms? Is most of your physical expression coming from your upper body—your head and your hands? Are you constantly restless?

Yes   No

Earth

Do you tend to slump in your chair? Is your physical movement slow and ponderous? Do you carry an air of hopelessness? Do you cross your arms tightly around your midriff? Do you gesticulate vaguely with your hands and wrists, allowing them to drop into your lap toward the end of the point you are making?

Yes   No

Metal

The extreme physical expression of a Metal imbalance is the lack of any movement. Do you keep very still? Do your shoulders stoop forward? Do you tend to curl up in a ball? Are you uncomfortable around others who gesticulate and express themselves wildly? Do you feel that you are in a shell?

Yes   No

VOICE

Our vocal expression changes from hour to hour and from day to day. The voice correlates to the health of the internal organs. Any obvious quality in the five examples below indicates an elemental imbalance. It is difficult to listen to your own voice, so you may need to tape record your voice and play it back. It would be wise to listen to those around you to get some practice in identifying the different voices. Again, a "Yes" answer in this section indicates a possible imbalance resulting from too much of one element.

Water

Does your voice sound wet, damp, weak? Does it sound like you are on the edge of tears, almost weeping?

Yes   No

Wood

Is your voice sharp, loud, and clear? Does it sound like you are shouting or arguing?

Yes   No

Fire

Is your vocal expression erratic? Does your voice go up and down, or do your sentences begin, stop, then begin? Does your voice sound like you are singing?

Yes   No

Earth

Is there a sense of incompletion in your vocal expression? Do you make a point and then meander off the point? Do you begin clearly and then your voice trails off, rather like sighing?

Yes   No

Metal

Is your voice rather dry and monotonous? Is there very little intonation in your speech? Is there an underlying presence of groaning?

Yes   No

Conclusion

Review the various answers that you circled and determine which element or elements are strongest. Be aware that this is representative only of who you are now and may not be representative of who you will be in the future or who you were in the past. Your condition is constantly changing.

Use your answers from the quiz along with your intuition as you read the descriptions below and see which element personality type (or types) sound most like you.

By the Numbers

Elemental personality types are also influenced by your birth year. Check out the following numbers to gain further insight into your element type.

You are likely to be a Fire personality type if your year of birth ends in the number six or seven. Red years (yang Fire) end in the number six: 1966, 1976, 1986, 1996, 2006, 2016, and so on. Purple years (yin Fire) end in the number seven: 1967, 1977, 1987, 1997, 2007, 2017, and so on.

You are likely to be an Earth personality type if your year of birth ends in the number eight or nine. Yellow years (yang Earth) end in the number eight: 1968, 1978, 1988, 1998, 2008, 2018, and so on. Gold years (yin Earth) end in the number nine: 1969, 1979, 1989, 1999, 2009, 2019, and so on.

You are likely to be a Metal personality type if the year of your birth ends in the number zero or one. White years (yang Metal) end in zero: 1960, 1970, 1980, 1990, 2000, 2010, and so on. Silver years (yin Metal) end in the number one: 1961, 1971, 1981, 1991, 2001, 2011, and so on.

You are likely to be a Water personality type if your year of birth ends in the number two or three. Black years (yang Water) end in the number two: 1962, 1972, 1982, 1992, 2002, 2012, and so on. Gray years (yin Water) end in the number three: 1963, 1973, 1983, 1993, 2003, 2013, and so on.

You are likely to be a Wood personality type if your birth year ends in the number four or five. Green years (yang Wood) end in the number four: 1964, 1974, 1984, 1994, 2004, 2014, and so on. Blue years (yin Wood) end in the number five: 1965, 1975, 1985, 1995, 2005, 2015, and so on.

The Fire Personality

Fire character traits are love, passion, leadership, spirituality, insight, dynamism, aggression, intuition, reason, and expressiveness. Common Fire emotions and qualities are excitement, joy, vanity, jealousy, frustration, regret, grief from loss of love, and disappointment in relationships. The Fire personality is direct—right out front. Are you funny and impulsive? Prone to becoming scattered? Known for your eclectic tastes? Do you enjoy decorating with unique art pieces and treasures from around the world? You may be a Fire personality.

Ways to Succeed

Your challenge is to share joy and laughter without the thought of reward. You may be tempted to indulge in arrogance, but you will succeed by becoming warmhearted and generous. Experiences of love, compassion, fun, joy, and pleasure are especially healing for you.

Fire

火

Fire is considered the most masculine of the five elements and is very yang. Even so, like all the elements, it has both a yin form as well as a yang form. When Fire expresses masculine yang energy, its color is red and it is symbolized by burning wood. When Fire expresses feminine yin energy, its color is purple and it is symbolized by the flame of a lamp.

- **Emotion:** Happiness

- **Planet:** Mars, the intense red planet

- **Chinese astrological signs:** Serpent, Horse, Sheep

- **Direction:** South

- **Season:** Summer, the time of heat, growth, warmth, and increased light

- **Climate:** Hot

- **Landscape form:** Peaked mountain

- **Building shape:** A pointed roof, such as an A-frame

- **Room:** The living room, where much activity takes place

- **Objects:** Any kind of lighting device including electric lights and lamps (but fluorescent bulbs deplete chi, whereas full-spectrum lightbulbs attract and maintain good chi), candles, oil lamps, natural sunlight, and fireplaces. Wild animals and domesticated pets, as well as animal parts, such as feathers, fur, wool, and bone.

> • **Symbol:** Red phoenix. Visual art that depicts fire, sunshine, or animals symbolizes fire, as do red colors, including purple, scarlet, magenta, hot pink, and orange.

The Earth Personality

Earth character traits are stability, practicality, reliability, industriousness, empathy, honesty, kindness, and prudence. Just as we take in nutrients through the stomach, we assimilate life experiences through the element Earth. Common Earth emotions and qualities are pensiveness, worry, thoughtfulness, instinctive awareness, and reflection. Do you value friendship and have a reputation for being kind, nurturing, and grounded? Do you love a comfortable, cozy room with thick rugs, stuffed furniture, and fancy decorations? Do you tend to collect too many objects and create clutter? When you are out of balance, do you start collecting and hoarding things, trying to get a sense of security by surrounding yourself with stuff? You may be an Earth personality.

Ways to Succeed

Your challenge is to honor your sympathetic nature and experience empathy with others, while also learning how to develop clear boundaries and take care of yourself. You will succeed by meditating and nourishing yourself physically, emotionally, and spiritually. A strong Earth element helps you to digest and accept fate and expand your circle of knowledge.

Earth

土

The element Earth is yin—feminine, like Mother Earth. When Earth expresses masculine yang energy, its color is yellow, and it is symbolized by a hill. When Earth expresses feminine yin energy, its color is gold, and it is symbolized by a valley.

- **Emotion:** Sympathy

- **Planet:** Saturn

- **Chinese astrological signs:** All twelve signs

- **Direction:** The center

- **Season:** The last eighteen days of each of the four seasons, the time of transition

- **Climate:** Damp

- **Landscape form:** A small mountain with a flat, tabletop peak

- **Building shape:** A flat roof and a square or rectangular structure

- **Room:** The dining room, where eating takes place

- **Objects:** All types of earthenware containers and vases, ceramic pieces, clay tiles, bricks, and adobe

- **Symbol:** The black and white yin-yang symbol. Visual art that depicts earthy landscapes, such as fields and natural environments, represent Earth, as do all yellow colors, including ochre and gold

The Metal Personality

Metal character traits include strength, independence, focus, intensity, righteousness, and fluency in speech. Common Metal emotions are gratitude, insecurity, inability to achieve parental expectations, or a lack of confidence. The Metal personality is very determined and powerful, with a tendency to be cool and reserved. Do you strive to create order in your environment, enjoying a room that is perfect and orderly? Do you prefer clean, minimalist design and dislike waste and excessive frilliness? You may be a Metal personality.

Ways to Succeed

Your challenge is to learn how to express grief and find healing. You will succeed by becoming less opinionated, accepting change, and gracefully releasing the past.

Metal

Metal is feminine (yin) because metal is extracted from the feminine earth (although Metal is considered less feminine than Earth or Water). When Metal expresses masculine yang energy, its color is white, and it is symbolized by a weapon. When metal expresses feminine yin energy, its color is silver, and it is symbolized by a kettle.

- **Emotion:** Gratitude when balanced, grief and insecurity when unbalanced

- **Planet:** Venus

- **Chinese astrological signs:** Monkey, Phoenix, Dog

- **Direction:** West

- **Season:** Autumn, the time of the harvest, completion, and the beginning of rest

- **Climate:** dry

- **Landscape form:** A lovely mountain with a gently curved peak, like a dome

- **Building shape:** A domed roof or an arch

- **Room:** The bedroom

- **Objects:** Sculptures made of metal ores, including silver, gold, brass, iron, aluminum, copper, tin, stainless steel, or metal alloys. Rocks, crystals, gems, and semiprecious stones are also considered to be Metal, not Earth, elements.

- **Symbol:** A white tiger. Visual art that is mostly white, silver, or light pastel in color represents metal.

The Water Personality

Water character traits are creativity, wisdom, sensitivity, reflection, persuasion, effectiveness, and desire for life and sex. Water types value family and social contacts and possess the ability to attract others. Are you seen as mysterious? Do you tend to internalize your feelings and think and ponder too much? Do you struggle with emotions such as fear, indecisiveness, vacilation, and uncertainty? Is your preference for a room that is dark and cool, a quiet place for rest? Do you seek ways to transform your bathroom into a nurturing environment for healing baths? You may be a water personality.

Ways to Succeed

Your challenge is to overcome your fears and become an active participant in life. You will succeed by not allowing fear to block the fullest expression of your creativity.

Water

Water is the most feminine of the five elements and therefore is considered very yin. In Taoist cosmology, femininity is not considered weak. On the contrary, Water is the most powerful element, for it can move around any obstacle in its path without losing its essential nature. Water can, in time, dissolve the hardest mountains. When Water expresses masculine yang energy, its color is black, and it is symbolized by a wave. When Water expresses feminine yin energy, its color is gray, and it is symbolized by a brook.

- **Emotion:** Wisdom and sensitivity when balanced, fear when unbalanced

- **Planet:** Mercury

- **Chinese astrological signs:** Boar, Rat, Ox

- **Direction:** North

- **Season:** Winter

- **Climate:** Cold

- **Landscape form:** Irregular peak, cupola (indented peaks), and watercourses on a peak

- **Building shape:** Detached houses, unusual architecture, irregular shapes, and one-of-a-kind dwellings, also dwellings where the front door or entrance is not easily visible

- **Room:** Bathroom

- **Objects:** All types of reflective surfaces, including mirrors, glass, and cut crystal. Pools, fountains, and aquariums.

- **Symbol:** A black tortoise. Visual art that is abstract or asymmetrical symbolizes Water, as do dark colors, including black, blue, and gray.

The Wood Personality

Wood character traits include good decision-making skills, idealism, imagination, compassion, and the ability to create change. Common Wood emotions are kindness, tension, criticism of self and others, discouragement, regret, and repressed anger related to thwarted affection. Do you find yourself often taking bold actions and initiating new projects? Are you focused, active, driven, and competitive? Do you appreciate the feelings of growth and expansion that come from a room full of lush plants and fresh flowers? You may be a Wood personality.

Ways to Succeed

Your challenge is to learn to transform anger into kindness and channel it into positive work that benefits all people. You will succeed by expressing your idealism and being a leader.

Wood

Wood is a masculine element considered less yang than Fire. When Wood expresses masculine yang energy, its color is green, and it is symbolized by a pine tree—sturdy, upright, and enduring. When Wood expresses feminine yin energy, its color is blue, and it is symbolized by the flexible bamboo that bends gently with the wind.

- **Emotion:** Anger

- **Planet:** Jupiter

- **Chinese astrological signs:** Tiger, Hare, Dragon

- **Direction:** East

- **Season:** Spring, the time of planting seeds, new growth, and beginnings

- **Climate:** Windy

- **Landscape form:** A mountain with a sharply rounded peak

- **Building shape:** A cylindrical structure like a silo

- **Room:** Kitchen

- **Objects:** Furniture and accessories made of wood; wood paneling and siding, decks and roofing; fabrics made of natural fibers such as cotton, hemp, and rayon; floral-patterned upholstery fabrics and wall coverings; all indoor and outdoor plants, including silk and plastic plants and flowers

- **Symbol:** An azure dragon. Visual art that depicts lush landscapes, gardens, plants, trees, and flowers symbolizes wood, as do all green and blue colors, including turquoise.

Feng Shui Cures

In Asia, furnishings and architecture are often designed with feng shui in mind. But Western art and architecture often has different criteria for design that can make balanced feng shui a challenge. Rooms may be missing significant guas, ceilings may be slanted, furniture may be awkwardly shaped. As a teen, you have the added challenge of not necessarily being in control of your furniture selection, finances, or decorating scheme. Like most things in life, your personal feng shui situation may not fit into a perfect, balanced package. Having trouble fitting all of your furniture in the proper guas and feeling like chi is getting blocked? Feng shui masters have been dealing with such dilemmas for centuries and have created a variety of feng shui cures.

Just as a doctor prescribes a course of treatment after diagnosing an illness, feng shui uses the energies of light, sound, movement, living things, weight, symbols, and water to cure various problems by increasing chi, decreasing chi, or redirecting chi.

Some of the most common cures include the addition of mirrors, plants, wind chimes, heavy objects like sculpture and stones, art, crystals, and incense and other scents. In this chapter you will find a description of some of the most common cures and special considerations for their use.

Remember to use your own creativity and intuition to apply cures to your specific situation. Note that the size of an item will determine the magnitude of the cure. Too large an item can create new problems if the new addition tips the scales of balance too far in another direction.

Feng shui uses the energies of light, sound, movement, living things, weight, symbols, and water to cure various problems by increasing chi, decreasing chi, or redirecting chi.

Mirrors

Mirrors can fix so many problems that they are jokingly called the aspirin of feng shui. They add lots of chi, light, and brightness. If you have a small space or a dark space, a mirror will do wonders to bring in more light and create a feeling of expansion. Oval or round mirrors are preferred to the sharp corners of square mirrors. Make sure that the glass on your mirror is not cloudy, smoky, chipped, or cracked, as that can distort the chi. If you want to go an extra step, there are many places that sell mirrors designed specifically for feng shui purposes. Typically, these are round mirrors that come in an eight-trigram frame. Don't be surprised if the trigram arrangement on these mirrors is different from the ba-gua map; it is an earlier form of the ba-gua.

A mirror is especially effective in the Relationships/Romance, Career, Creativity/Children, and Helpful people/Travel guas. But a mirror is not recommended for the Wealth gua—money might come your way, but will quickly be reflected right out of your hands. It is not wise to place a mirror in the Fame/Reputation (Fire) gua because a mirror is a symbol of water, which extinguishes fire.

Full-length mirrors should not cut off your head or feet. Hang smaller circular mirrors at the proper height to reflect your face. If you have grown and the mirror is still where you placed it three years ago, when you were six inches shorter, make sure to bring the mirror up to your current height.

Plants

If mirrors are the aspirin of feng shui, plants are like the healing salve. Plants offer vital chi, represent the Wood element, and provide lots of oxygen while adding beauty and connecting us to the natural world. They can soften the hard edges of a bedroom feature, muffle traffic noise, and offer emotional comfort. Fresh flowers and lush plants are symbolic of fresh ideas, and new mental and spiritual growth. Flowers can also bring good luck. Choose flowering plants with colors that correspond to the energy you are hoping to attract (shown in the color guide on page 65), or plants that emit a smell you like. Be sure to choose plants with leaves that are rounded, offering soothing yin energy, not pointed, spiky, leaves like a cactus.

Plants must be healthy. An unhealthy plant in a gua of your room can block chi flow in that area of your life. If you do not have a green thumb, use fresh or silk flowers. Match the color of the flowers to the colors of the gua or element.

Wind Chimes, Bells, Music, and Other Sounds

Sound can add positive chi while simultaneously dispersing sha chi. Wind chimes are the most popular form of using sound for stimulating the flow of chi. Wind chimes are best placed where a breeze can move them. Be sure to choose a wind chime that makes a sound you love to hear and that is in tune. Metal tube chimes are best, not wood, shell, glass, or other materials.

Mobiles

Mobiles are a wonderful way to create motion in an indoor room. Mobiles serve a similar purpose to wind chimes. They circulate chi in lifeless areas where there is little motion. Mobiles are very effective at livening up a corner. If you wish to add a mobile to a gua, find one with colors and symbols that are appropriate to that gua. For example, a pink mobile of objects in pairs is perfect for the Relationships/Romance gua.

Heavy Objects

Large smooth rocks and other heavy objects made of stone or porcelain are useful to add emphasis or stablilize energy in a gua. Heavy objects are particularly useful in rooms that were once attics or garages to help ground the space. This also applies to penthouses, rooms with skylights, and any space where there is a floating feeling. Avoid the use of any heavy objects that are jagged as they create chaos.

Art

Select your art carefully. Be sure that the first thing seen when you enter your room is uplifting and inspiring. This sets the tone for the entire room. Most abstract art is chaotic and not recommended. If you have loud, fiery art place it in the Fame/Reputation gua. When placing art, always consider colors that correspond to each gua (see color guide on page 65).

Chinese art depicts a great variety of imagery. One common theme is the landscape, which is usually lush, rich, and mountainous. Landscapes are considered particularly fortunate images to have in the Knowledge gua. Scrolls or paintings of fish are superb in the Wealth gua. Images of flowers or ducks in pairs work well in the Relationships/Romance gua. Flowers are also a popular theme for Chinese art. Such images are a wonderful way to introduce plants to the room if you do not have a green thumb.

Crystals

Crystals are feng shui enhancements that offer spiritual blessing and cheer wherever they are placed because of their capacity to enhance chi and break

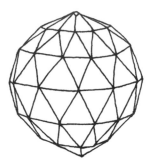

A crystal ball is a powerful feng shui cure.

up sha chi. An example of this is how a prism refracts the harsh rays of the sun into a rainbow.

The crystals recommended for feng shui cures are not the kind that are rough, with sharp edges. Feng shui crystals are leaded glass crystal balls that are carefully cut to be multifaceted and reflect light from all directions. Crystal balls perform at their best when hung in windows where they can absorb new light and refract it into all corners of your room. They break up any overactive chi coming from the outside while cheering up darker spaces. A crystal can also be placed in a holder on a desk or tabletop. To add even more positive chi, hang your crystal ball on a 9-inch red ribbon. Red symbolizes life, vitality, and abundant chi. Nine is a very powerful number in feng shui because it is the highest and most yang of all the single digits. If 9 inches is too short for your purposes, hang the crystal on a red string that is a multiple of nine. Eighteen inches is usually long enough to catch light in a window.

Scent and Incense

What's the first thing that you smell when you walk into your room? If the scent is sweet or inviting, you immediately feel good about being there. If the smell is uninviting, you may want to consider aromatherapy. First remove from your room or put away anything stinky: shoes, fish bowls, sheets in need of washing, gym clothes, strong paints, smoke, or old food—they all have the capacity to pack quite an olfactory punch. Then you can get creative with the feel of your environment. Incenses, perfumes, aromatic candles, and oil dispensers are wonderful ways to establish mood. The most effective smell is a subtle, pleasing one, so be sure to not go overboard. Any herbal shop will offer numerous varieties of scents to evoke ambience. Calming scents are derived from the oils of most flowers and fruits including chamomile, rose, orange, and grapefruit. Healing scents include clary sage, juniper, and eucalyptus. Cleansing scents include lavender, basil, and tea tree. Lavender is also excellent for general relaxation and meditation.

Different methods of scent production may have different benefits and risks. Candles are wonderful but, when left unattended, can be the cause of household fires. Many candle companies use synthetic chemicals to produce scents—these chemicals are bad for you, bad for the environment, and often overpowering in their potency. If you love candles, use beeswax candles or candles made with pure essential oils.

Oil dispensers work by placing a small amount of aromatic oil into a container. The container is filled with a bit of water to distill the scent and prevent the oil from burning. The oil is heated by tea light candles. Oils can also be used to scent bathtubs, sachets for your drawers, or your body. There are also aromatherapy dispensers that plug into an electric socket and steadily release a scent. These can be left unattended and can be quite effective in steadily releasing aroma.

Incense can come in the form of a stick or a cone or even a powder that gets burned on top of charcoal. Incense quality varies. While cost is not always an indicator of quality, it does make some sense to beware of cheap incense such as ash burning sticks sprayed with perfume. These smoke more heavily and their scent is less smooth and subtle. Other options for scent are fresh scented flowers—such as the stargazer lily—and flowering house plants.

Lucky Symbols

Feng shui lore has many lucky symbols that can be used to bring good luck to a gua. These include:

- **Dragon:** This mythical animal represents the Emperor of China, power, great fortune, and virtue of character. Dragons work well in all guas, especially the Family/Health area. But if you are born in the year of the Dog, it will not be lucky for you to use the Dragon symbol because Dragon is opposite Dog in Chinese astrology.

- **Three-Legged Frog:** This funny-looking frog sits on a pile of gold coins and symbolizes big money. It can be placed in your Wealth corner or near a cash register for a business.

- **Fu dogs:** Fu dogs are stylized Chinese lions that represent power and prestige. A pair of large stone fu dogs are used at the entrances of buildings to provide protection.

- **Bat:** The bat is thought to bring good fortune and happiness. Two bats symbolize double happiness.

- **Crane:** This lovely delicate bird represent long life and wisdom.

- **Fish:** Fish represent money and abundance in feng shui. Because the carp swims upstream, it also symbolizes perseverance and success.

- **Phoenix:** This magical bird represents the Empress of China, peace, and blessings. This is especially lucky to use if you are born in Phoenix year.

Some have already been mentioned in preceding chapters. Some people prefer to create their own lucky symbols based on images that carry personal significance.

Common Problems

Below are some of the more common problems that people experience when applying feng shui principles to their room.

Missing or Incomplete Guas

You may have discovered, when you first mapped out your room, on page 39, that your room is missing a gua or that a particular gua is a little smaller than the rest. A gua will also be incomplete if slanted ceilings or dormers cut into a space lower than the height of your head so that you cannot comfortably walk in that gua. In all of these instances, you can compensate for the loss of chi. Add chi to these areas through light, motion, sound, or plants. An effective cure for adding chi to a gua with a slanted ceiling is to hang a string of white Christmas tree lights along the crease of where the wall meets the ceiling. Make sure to keep it neat by fastening the lights securely so that the lights do not droop or hang unevenly. Another cure is to hang a crystal on a 9-inch red cord.

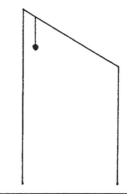

Is My Room Too Yin?

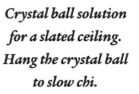

Crystal ball solution for a slated ceiling. Hang the crystal ball to slow chi.

Excessive yin can slow you down and be depressing and depleting. Too much yin can be caused by low ceilings, angled ceilings, little light, and dark colors. The first step to take is to look at the colors in your room and figure out how to brighten them. Since the bedroom should be a restful place when you do want to sleep, the ideal way to add yang color is through splashes. Rather than paint your entire wall bright red and yellow, consider shades of soft white and pastels for the walls and add bright, dynamic accent colors through pillows, window coverings, and artwork.

Lights add both brightness and heat, which are yang qualities, so add lights where possible to enhance yang chi. Check your window covers: are they heavy, dark colors that block out the natural yang sunlight? You can add yang energy by replacing heavy curtains with lighter drapes of brighter colors that still block glare and provide privacy while letting in the sunlight.

You can also create more yang chi by airing out your room. Open your windows for a while. If you live somewhere warm, air out your room with fresh air at least once each day. Heating bills in cold climates will discourage you from applying this strategy in wintry zones. If you live in a cold climate you can still keep air circulating in your room by keeping a window open a bit for a little while each day.

If you can keep your windows open and get an occasional breeze, it is

Heavy, dark window covers will be oppressive and create too much yin, like a cave.

Transform your bedroom with lighter window coverings that allow for privacy while letting the natural sunlight into the room.

wonderful to place a small wind chime in the center of your window. Another option to increase chi is to hang a small bell on your door that will offer a gentle ringing every time the door opens and closes.

Too Much Yang!

Can't seem to settle down to do your homework? Your room may have too much yang chi. If you're the type of person that does many activities at once, including listening to loud music while talking on the phone and playing computer games, chances are there is excessive yang chi in your room. Your room may also be too yang if it experiences constant exposure to sunlight or if you live in a city where bright streetlights or lights from other buildings come into your room. Too many bright, primary colors or clashing patterns can also create overwhelming yang. Too much yang energy causes restlessness and the inability to concentrate. Ironically, most public schools are too yang, with their florescent lighting and stark combinations of tile floors and cement walls. Add to that the sounds of slamming lockers and the constant motion of students racing between classes and its no wonder that people would prefer to be socializing (a very yang activity) than sitting at a desk studying (yin).

Whenever possible, add circular patterns and shapes to balance straight, hard lines.

The best cure for a yang-excessive environment is the introduction of the element of Water. Water is extremely yin. Gentle fountains, or posters of soothing water images are easy ways to introduce the water element to your space. Gentle blue or green hues are watery by nature. Another way to reduce yang chi is by softening some of the colors in your room. Consider soft off-whites and pastels with a matte finish rather than glaring whites or bright primary colors. Make sure all of your lights are covered by soft lampshades and avoid heavy fluorescent lighting. For even more yin energy, install a dimmer switch, or use lightbulbs with lower wattage.

Poison Arrows

Sharp edges of furniture can cause poison arrows—sharp energy lines that dart out invisibly and cut right through chi. These poison arrows can be absorbed by placing plants, lights, drapes, or mirrors over the sharp edges. Whenever possible, add circular or rounded patterns, shapes, and objects in your space, such as oval rugs or round mirrors, to balance straight, hard lines.

The mouth of chi can be seen in the reflection of the mirror.

No Way to Place the Bed in the Commanding Position

Sometimes the bed can go *either* deep into the room *or* so that you can see the mouth of chi, but not *both*. You can solve this problem by placing a mirror diagonally from the bed so that you can see the mouth of chi through the mirror.

Desk Is Placed So That Your Back Is Facing the Mouth of Chi

It is desirable to be facing the mouth of chi. Working with your back to the door is a very vulnerable position and is not fortunate. You can resolve this by placing a small round mirror at head level along the wall that your desk is facing so that you can see all movement at the mouth of chi.

A Primary Object or Activity Is in the Coffin Position

Does your bed or any primary activity occur in the coffin position discussed on page 53? You can slow the chi as it enters your room by placing a circular rug in front of your bed. You can also hang a crystal ball between the door and the bed. Placing a footboard or chest at the foot of your bed will also block oncoming chi. The same strategies can be applied to other primary activities—such as studying at a desk—that take place in the coffin position.

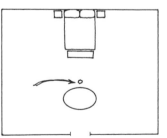

You can combine a rug, crystal, and footboard to slow down chi. This is desirable when your bed is in the coffin position.

15

Chinese Astrology: The Timing of Your Life

So what does it mean if you've pulled all of these hints and tips together and yet you're still not noticing results? You've cleared your room of clutter, you've unblocked your mouth of chi and witness chi moving freely throughout the room, your objects are all placed in the correct guas. You've utilized color, light, sound, smell, and other cures to balance yin and yang and elemental flow of chi. And yet, you're still feeling blocked in your life. Don't panic. It's probably not your feng shui practice. The answer lies in astrological timing.

Your Astrological Timing

No matter how much you wish to mold and shape your life, there are larger currents that influence your situation. Chinese astrology can offer insight into the currents that shape your path. While a thorough astrological interpretation can only be provided by an established astrologer, you can read this chapter to learn the basics of Chinese astrology and make some simple feng shui decisions to support your Chinese astrological sign.

Twelve Chinese Animals

You probably already know your Western astrology sign: be it Aries the Ram, Taurus the Bull, Gemini the Twins, Cancer the Crab, Leo the Lion, Virgo the Virgin, Libra the Scales, Scorpio the Scorpion (or Eagle), Sagittarius the Archer, Capricorn the Goat, Aquarius the Water Bearer, or Pisces the Fishes.

Chinese astrology is not based on the month you were born. Instead, your Chinese sign is based on the year you were born. That is why most of your friends and almost all of your classmates will be the same Chinese sign as you are. You have a natural compatibility because you all are the same sign. When your teen years are over and you go out in the world and interact with many types of people, you will notice that relating isn't as easy as it is now with your friends. That's because new people probably aren't your same sign. A common reason for problems with relatives is that they are not a compatible Chinese sign. Know your sign and plan accordingly, especially if you plan to have children in a few years or later in life.

What's Your Sign?

Discover your astrology sign by finding your year of birth on the following chart. The Chinese New Year is never January 1st. Instead, it is the second new moon after winter solstice, which falls around February 5th. Notice that each sign repeats every twelve years.

Rat: 1984, 1996, 2008, 2020, etc., every twelve years.

Ox: 1985, 1997, 2009, 2021

Tiger: 1986, 1998, 2010, 2022

Hare: 1987, 1999, 2011, 2023

Dragon: 1988, 2000, 2012, 2024

Serpent: 1989, 2001, 2013, 2025

Horse: 1990, 2002, 2014, 2026

Sheep: 1991, 2003, 2015, 2027

Monkey: 1980, 1992, 2004, 2016, 2028

Phoenix: 1981, 1993, 2005, 2017, 2029

Dog: 1982, 1994, 2006, 2018, 2030

Boar: 1983, 1995, 2007, 2019, 2031

Teen Rat

In Chinese astrology, rats are not vermin to be exterminated. Instead, Rat is smart, clever, really sharp, and a survivor. You are lucky to be a Rat because Rat is number one in all things and is extremely intelligent. You and your friends are very close, like a Rat pack. Rats are often bored in school because they are so smart that they quickly understand educational material and desire more creative stimulation. So it is up to each Rat to find creative projects and challenges. A lazy Rat is a lost Rat. Most Rats are clean, conscientious, and tidy. But if you are a Rat who loves to hoard and collect too much stuff, be sure to reduce your clutter or you will block your own good fortune.

Rat Tale

A Chinese folktale tells how the Rat became the first animal of the Chinese zodiac. In ancient times, a contest was planned in a village to select the twelve astrology animals. All the animals were excited and wanted to be included. After hearing news of this contest, Rat went to visit Ox on a neighboring farm where Ox toiled and plowed the fields. Rat convinced Ox to travel to the contest. Could Rat ride on Ox's back to the village? Rat doesn't weigh much, and Ox would enjoy Rat's company. So Ox trudged over vast terrain with Rat riding high on his back. Ox swam a mighty river with Rat hanging on to his back.

As soon as they arrived at the village, Rat quickly jumped off Ox's back, scurried in, and arrived first. In this way, clever Rat was made number one and Ox became number two. In the Buddhist version of this Rat tale, the animal that was first to the bedside of the dying Buddha would be made the first zodiac animal. Clever Rat was first. He scurried in after he used Ox for transport.

Rat Friends and Foes

Teen Rat is most compatible with other Rats and those born in the year of the Dragon and Monkey. Rat, Dragon, and Monkey like to live large and accomplish much in life. Rat is also compatible with steady Ox, even though Rat outwitted Ox to become the first animal of the zodiac. Ox is reliable and dependable, offering Rat needed stability. Rat is least compatible with Horse, Rat's opposite. Horse's carefree and rebellious attitude could aggravate the thrifty and cautious Rat. Horse years are usually not lucky for Rat. Instead, Rat is lucky in Rat, Ox, Dragon, Serpent, and Monkey years. These lucky years are best for marriage or having a child. Select a pet born in one of these years to be harmonious with your animal.

Rat Life Areas

Teen life choice areas for Rat should emphasize Knowledge, Career, and Wealth. Knowledge is important because Rat thrives on learning, succeeding, and excelling in all things. The Career area matters because Rat wants to attain victory and have work that brings fulfillment. And money matters to any Rat, who is good with money. Rats often accumulate wealth as a result of being the first in all things and applying their Rat ingenuity and intelligence. Should a Rat tend to hoard, consistently remove clutter from all areas.

Teen Ox

牛 Ox is solid, dependable, and hard working. If this sounds boring, be glad that you are an Ox because you will make something of your self in this lifetime. And you will do it through your own creativity and hard work. Oxen are best when they follow through with their duties, commit to school projects, plan goals, and then work steadily to achieve them. Like oxen plowing a field, Ox will work hard, but an abundant harvest is the result. Slow and steady wins the race. In schoolwork and all areas of creative expression, including sports, Ox can be a strong, uncontested winner. Oxen are reliable and realistic about their goals and aspirations.

Ox Tale

According to ancient Chinese legend, humans have a special relationship with Ox. In early agricultural communities, people often went for days without eating and feared starvation. To aid suffering humans, the gods and goddesses removed Ox from heaven, where she was a star, and sent her to earth. The divine ones instructed Ox to tell people that with her help they would avoid starvation and eat every three days. Ox misunderstood and told humanity that they would eat three times a day. Ox had to make her words true, and that is why Ox must labor so hard for people and endure many burdens without complaint.

Ox Friends and Foes

Teen Ox is most compatible with other Oxen and those born in the year of the Serpent and Phoenix (Rooster). All are hard working, mature, and dependable. Ox also favors Rat, who offers Ox clever solutions. Ox is least compatible with Sheep, Ox's opposite. Capricious Sheep may be too changeable and inconstant for reliable Ox. Sheep years are usually not lucky for Ox. Instead, Ox is lucky in Ox, Rat, Serpent, and Phoenix years. These lucky years are best for marriage or having a child. Select a pet born in one of these years to be harmonious with your animal.

Ox Life Areas

Teen life choice areas for honest Ox should emphasize stability in the Career and Family/Health areas. Ox diligently applies much energy to completing tasks. This strong attitude helps Ox when they choose a life career. Family security is also important to Ox, who can be a bit traditional, so the Family/Health area should not be neglected. Ox tends to be the family peacemaker and shoulder responsibilities. If this becomes too overwhelming, clear out and then embellish the Family/Health area.

Teen Tiger

虎 Tiger is strong, mighty, dynamic, and lives life with much gusto and vitality. Tiger teens have many interests, are often active in sports, and feel that they have much to accomplish during their teen years. They are very quick, usually too quick for their teachers to understand, unless their teacher happens to also be born in a Tiger year. In some instances, Tigers can be like wild tigers with a bad temper, especially teen males. To conform to school lessons, do homework, and obey parental demands can seem like the Tiger is in a cage. But once Tiger survives and thrives during their teen years, they can spend the rest of their lives as free souls and do as their lust for life personality desires. Don't be shy! Roar, Tiger, roar.

Tiger Tale

Mighty Tiger was hunting in the jungle one night when he was caught in a net trap. Before he knew what happened, he was swinging from a high branch, unable to move. He roared and roared. A Rat was out looking for something to eat when he heard the roaring. Tiger saw the little Rat and cried out, "Please, Rat, scurry up here and gnaw these ropes so I can be free." Rat realized that the thick ropes required more than one set of teeth, so he went home and got his wife and sixty-four children. Together the entire family scurried up the tree and gnawed until daylight.

Mighty Tiger fell free of his ropes just as the sun was rising. Usually a Tiger would never eat little rodents like rats. But he was hungry after swinging in the tree all night. So with one great swipe of his Tiger paw, the Rat family was devoured in one gulp.

Tiger Friends and Foes

Teen Tiger is most compatible with other Tigers and those born in the years of the Horse and the Dog. All like excitement, travel, and new endeavors and challenges. Tiger also favors the Boar because Boar offers the sensuality, creativity, and affection that Tiger desires. Tiger is least compatible with Monkey, Tiger's opposite. Antagonistic Monkey can tease (pull Tiger's tail) resulting in Tiger's anger. Monkey years are usually not lucky for Tiger. Instead, Tiger is lucky in Tiger, Horse, Dog, and Boar years. These lucky years are best for marriage or having a child. Select a pet born in one of these years to be harmonious with your animal.

Tiger Life Areas

Teen life choice area for inquisitive Tiger should definitely emphasize two areas: Creativity and Knowledge. Creativity is required to encourage development of artistic personal expression. A Tiger who is not free to express creatively will feel thwarted. Because Tiger can act impulsively without reflection, embellishment of the Knowledge area is necessary. Many Tigers are not scholarly, so it can be easy to neglect this important area. But if Knowledge is addressed, Tiger can better understand why they react in confining situations or rebel against doing their schoolwork.

Teen Hare

The gentle qualities of springtime are traits of those born in Hare years. Hares love art, peace, and beauty. They are usually fashion conscious and have refined tastes; often more refined than most adults. A class of teen Hares is easier than most other students because Hares dislike fighting and difficulties. They enjoy classes that are not competitive and appreciate when classroom circumstances are pleasant. Hare does not want to fight. Instead, Hare wishes to enjoy life, and especially enjoy the company of friends. Some Hares can be a bit shy and not strongly pursue their goals. Try to enjoy your teen years. You have the rest of your life to achieve what you want.

Hare Tale

The Chinese legend of the moon goddess Ch'ang-o is associated with the Hare. Ch'ang-o was the wife of an archer named Ki. Brave Ki shot down ten suns when the suns rose together to scorch the earth. Although Ki was courageous, he was a ruthless man. In reward for shooting the suns, Ki was given a brew of immortality. One day when Ki was out hunting, Ch'ang-o drank his brew in an attempt to stop his cruelty. When Ki returned and realized what happened, he tried to kill Ch'ang-o, but she escaped to the moon and was protected by the moon Hare. Afraid to return to earth, Ch'ang-o lived happily with the moon Hare and became a sacred moon goddess and protector of children. (Hare's lunar connection is that it takes 28 days, one lunar month, before newborn Hares are ready to leave their mother.)

Hare Friends and Foes

Teen Hare is most compatible and content with other Hares and those born in the year of the Sheep and Boar. These three astrology signs are easygoing and appreciate the arts. Hare also favors Dogs, whose trust, loyalty, protection, and eagerness to help Hare are sincerely valued. Hare is least compatible with Phoenix, Hare's opposite. The blunt, sometimes critical Phoenix communication can feel like a bludgeoning beak on the Hare's thin skin. Phoenix years are usually not lucky for Hare. Instead, lucky years for Hare are Hare, Sheep, Dog, and Boar years. These lucky years are best for marriage or having a child. Select a pet born in one of these years to be harmonious with your animal.

Hare Life Areas

Teen life choice area for peace-loving Hare should emphasize the Relationships/Romance gua because Hare desires refinement and harmony in all interactions with others. Hare can become upset, even ill, when others do not behave in a gracious and harmonious manner—especially vulgar parents. By cultivating the peaceful qualities of like-minded companions, Hare can create a charmed circle of close friends, classmates, and romantic partners.

Teen Dragon

龍

The Chinese Dragon is the most powerful and magnificent creature of the Chinese zodiac. It is nothing like the Western concept of the vile dragon, a scaly beast to be slayed by knights and saints. Instead, Dragon is the symbol of royalty, prosperity, wisdom, vitality, and benevolence. If you are born in the year of the Dragon, you are most fortunate. You are born to lead and accomplish great things. Because of Dragon's power, your life experiences are intense. It is as if you are living ten lifetimes in this one current incarnation. When do you get to turn down the volume? You don't. This is how your life will be; full of daring, drama, bravery, and excitement. You will cover much ground and be able to travel the world, like a dragon flying across the heavens. But regal Dragons must make their dreams a reality, and not get lost in a cloud, expecting the hard work to be done by others.

Dragon Tale

Dragon is a shamanic animal who can shrink to the size of a silkworm and then instantly swell until it fills the space between heaven and earth. There are many magical Dragons in Chinese mythology. A heavenly Dragon guarantees that life continues on earth. A spirit Dragon brings rain. An earth Dragon (of feng shui) rules mountains, rivers, and waterfalls. A sea Dragon lives in a splendid palace full of beautiful and rare treasures. Lucky humans can visit his castle at the bottom of the sea. There they are rewarded with treasures, even offered one of his daughters in marriage, and given the five life blessings of wealth, long life, peace, virtue, and good health.

Dragon Friends and Foes

Teen Dragon is most compatible with other Dragons and those born in the year of the Rat and Monkey. All are smart, sharp, intense, and strong animal signs. Dragon also favors Phoenix because they make a harmonious pair whose vital energies are well matched. Together, Dragon and Phoenix are a symbol of marriage. Dragon is least compatible with Dog who is Dragon's opposite. No-nonsense Dog is too realistic to believe in Dragon's dreams or to flatter Dragon's big ego. Dog years are not lucky for Dragon. Instead, Dragon is lucky in Rat, Dragon, Monkey, and Phoenix years. These lucky years are best for marriage or having a child. Select a pet born in one of these years to be harmonious with your animal.

Dragon Life Areas

Teen life choice areas for mighty Dragon should emphasize fame and include the color red. Powerful Dragon desires acclaim and respect from everyone who orbits in their world. An illustrious career is also important for Dragon. Even though Dragon may change careers because there is so much to see and do as a Dragon, these career changes are often also advancements for the life path of the Dragon. If a dead-end career should occur, it won't last long. As a basic feng shui principle, Dragon must not live in clutter and should weed out clothes from their overwhelming wardrobe.

Teen Serpent

蛇

In Chinese cosmology, Serpents are not evil scary creatures. Serpents are wise, beautiful, intelligent, and psychologically complex. As a teen Serpent, you will not be interested in superficial activities. Instead, your interactions with others must have meaning. Most teen Serpents possess a depth of character, seem wise beyond their years, and are more sexually sophisticated than other teens. But you must not allow your introspective and contemplative nature to become moody, demanding, or mean.

Serpent Tale

The Chinese classic tale tells of a 1,000-year-old serpent that practiced magic and transformed herself into a beautiful young woman. Through her charms, she married a scholar, made him wealthy, and her life was happy and content. But when the Serpent beauty became pregnant, a Taoist monk persuaded the scholar that his wife was not human. The monk was an expert at capturing shape-shifting animals who falsely assumed human forms. Wise Serpent outwitted him many times before he finally exposed her dual lives. The monk confined the Serpent beauty to a lovely pagoda by a lake. Her son grew up to be a famous scholar who visited his Serpent mother whom he loved deeply.

Serpent Friends and Foes

Serpent is most compatible with other Serpents and those born in the year of the Ox and Phoenix. They possess similar values and goals. Serpent also favors Monkey because Serpent's wisdom coupled with Monkey's guile can create an unbeatable team. Serpent is least compatible with Boar, Serpent's opposite. The calculating, psychological Serpent might find Boar to be too simple and basic. Boar years are not lucky for Serpent. Instead, Serpent is lucky in Serpent, Ox, Monkey, and Phoenix years. These lucky years are best for marriage or having a child. Select a pet born in one of these years to be harmonious with your animal.

Serpent Life Areas

Teen life choice area for contemplative Serpent should emphasize knowledge. If this area of life is cultivated, wise Serpent can develop the innate self-awareness to act properly during any life challenge. To create a void in which to place new understanding—the hollow cave of the mountain—Serpent must shed the skins of the past. The Family/Health area is also important for Serpent because the shedding of skin symbolizes the next generation and the importance of what we learn from our elders that we pass on to our children. The Fame/Reputation area must be controlled and modulated for summer-born Serpents to curb ruthless behavior. Serpents must remove clutter often. They tend to place clutter on stairways and block the entry to rooms, creating an environment that only a serpent can slither through to enter.

Teen Horse

Horse is a free spirit who wants to race throughout life with the energy of a wild horse. Horse is bright, open, cheerful, athletic, naturally popular, and attracts many friends. Horse creates their own herd of like-minded souls who enjoy life and celebrate the good things that life has to offer. Horses are strong, direct, and tell you exactly what is on their mind. They dislike weak, wishy-washy people. They prefer to solve problems quickly and easily. Horses are instinctive animals, so those born in a Horse year are also instinctive and highly intuitive. Follow your hunches. Your keen judgment and instincts can help you make the right decisions throughout your life. One difficult Horse trait is rebelliousness. Because of Horse's carefree nature, you need ample room for self-expression. When constrained by rules, proud Horse refuses to be corralled or tamed. Stay free Horse, stay free!

Horse Tale

Powerful Horse is the hero of Chinese history. Great dynasties expanded and wars were won thanks to the Horse, which is revered in China. Famous generals are known for their brave and devoted Horses. Many Chinese military stories and legends are of Horses who determined the outcomes of important battles. One Horse tale tells of the Chinese warrior Liu Bei. He discovered a plot to assassinate him so he fled on his Horse. After crossing a shallow lake, the Horse became stuck in deep mud and could not move. The pursing assassins approached. Liu Bei spoke to his Horse, as if the animal could understand, asking his Horse to move because their lives were in danger. The Horse responded and used his great strength to jump out of the mud and outrun the assassins. In this classic story, part of historical lore, the hero is not Liu Bei. The hero is his Horse.

Horse Friends and Foes

Horse is most compatible with other Horses and those born in the year of the Tiger and Dog. Together they have fun adventures and take risks in life. Horse also appreciates the gentility, charm, and beauty of Sheep, who is willing to forgive Horse her selfishness. Horse is least compatible with Rat, Horse's opposite. Horse's need for freedom and variety may not always be understood by materialist, practical Rat. Rat years are not lucky for Horse. Instead, Horse is lucky in Horse, Tiger, Sheep, and Dog years. These lucky years are best for marriage or having a child. Select a pet born in one of these years to be harmonious with your animal.

Horse Life Areas

Teen life choice area for expressive Horse should emphasize Creativity/Children to help Horse have more fun and enjoy life in a free, childlike manner. Horse often succeeds after others intervene to offer guidance, so focus on the Helpful people/Travel area is also important, especially during the teen years. If you are the type of Horse who is too impulsive or temperamental, you will benefit greatly from developing the Knowledge area to figure out why and when you get out of control.

Teen Sheep

Sheep's core nature is artistic, kind, and gentle. You love peace, creativity, and harmony. For a career, Sheep succeeds in the arts because Sheep appreciates beauty and is the connoisseur of all life has to offer. Good-hearted Sheep is very intuitive, a good listener, and is extremely empathetic. Gentle and graceful, Sheep easily charms people by making them feel special. Sheep is often deeply spiritual with a strong interest in metaphysics and the occult. Sheep's kindness does not indicate a weak character. Sheep is calm in appearance yet strong in determination. The teen years are often challenging for Sheep. As Sheep ages, life becomes better. While Sheep usually struggles in youth, in old age Sheep has good things and is surrounded by loving family and friends and comfortable circumstances. One impulsive Sheep trait is the tendency to overindulge in beautiful things. "Sheep eat paper," meaning that Sheep often overspend on luxury and artifice.

Sheep Tale

In Chinese fairy tales and legends, Sheep are friendly to humans and want to help them. To do this, Sheep are able to change shape and turn into jade or stone. In one story, a flock of Sheep approached a riverbank. There they turned into stones to be used to construct a bridge. In another story, a young shepherd went to study with a Taoist priest in the mountains. When the shepherd did not return, his father inquired about his son's welfare. The priest brought the father to where the shepherd was meditating and learning Taoist magic. The father saw that there were very many white stones near the cave where his son meditated. When the shepherd saw his father, he cried out, "Rise, Sheep." The white stones stood up and turned into a huge flock of Sheep, all gifts for his father.

Sheep Friends and Foes

Sheep is most compatible with another kindred soul Sheep, and those born in the year of the Hare and Boar. They are gentle folk who enjoy the arts and the finer things in life. Sheep also enjoys the companionship of Horse, whose optimistic disposition helps Sheep be less pessimistic. Sheep is least compatible with Ox, Sheep's opposite. Sheep's artistic sensibilities could judge Ox as dull and too conservative. Ox years are not lucky for Sheep. Instead, Sheep is lucky in Hare, Horse, Sheep, and Boar years. These lucky years are best for marriage or having a child. Select a pet born in one of these years to be harmonious with your animal.

Sheep Life Areas

Teen life area choices for kind and gentle Sheep should emphasize overall balance of all eight guas. Being a peaceful flock animal, the Relationships/ Romance area is important to the Sheep individual. Sheep have a natural capacity to understand their role in the Family/Health gua because lambs demonstrate correct reverence for elders when they kneel before their mother to nurse. Sheep also have an affinity for the Knowledge area because Sheep enjoy solitary reflective moments to restore their soul and find peace. Sheep who feel a bit lost during their teen years are bettered when the Helpful people/Travel area is strengthened, as they benefit from positive guidance.

Teen Monkey

You are lucky if you are born in the year of the Monkey, one of the favored animals of Chinese astrology. Don't think that a Monkey is in any way ape-like or below humans. Monkeys are very talented and have natural abilities in many areas. They are artistic, creative, good with their hands, and quick with computers. In short, Monkey can do anything! They are smart as well as strong. Monkeys are leaders and must learn to tolerate weaker siblings and not dominate others. Because fun Monkey is so intelligent, Monkeys can suffer from "monkey mind": jump to a branch, peel a banana, take a bite, drop it; jump to the next branch, peel a banana, take a bite, drop it . . . on and on in a useless cycle. Teen Monkeys must temper the issue of boredom and lack of discipline and not succumb to Monkey mind.

Monkey Tale

A long time ago, a special magical Monkey was born with supernatural abilities. Soon he was crowned King of the Monkeys. This magical Monkey was smart but overconfident of his tricks. He was so fearless and arrogant that he even challenged Buddha. He bet that Buddha would never be able to catch him. Magical Monkey jumped on a cloud and traveled to a place thousands of miles away. When he came upon a five-peaked mountain, he took a rest. While he happily congratulated himself for outsmarting Buddha, the five mountain peaks suddenly turned into Buddha's five fingers.

Monkey Friends and Foes

Monkey is most compatible with other Monkeys and those born in the year of the Rat and Dragon. They are go-getters who want to experience what life has to offer. Monkey is also compatible with wise Serpent because Serpent understands the Monkey mind and can use it to their mutual advantages. Monkey is least compatible with Tiger, Monkey's opposite. Tiger years are not lucky for Monkey. Instead, Monkey is lucky in Rat, Dragon, Serpent, and Monkey years. These lucky years are best for marriage or having a child. Select a pet born in one of these years to be harmonious with your animal.

Monkey Life Areas

Teen life choice areas for Monkey should emphasize Fame/Reputation. Embellishments in this gua include much use of the color red. Individualist Monkey is successful in life and can achieve great accomplishments regardless of obstacles. The more fame and recognition that inspired Monkeys receive for their wild schemes and innovative concepts, the more they are inspired to achieve and create. Also of importance is the Career area. Monkeys apply more of their ingenious wit and dynamic energy to a career that they find personally satisfying.

Teen Phoenix

鳳

Phoenixes are very special because their lives are cycles of rebirths, just like a Phoenix rising anew from the flames of transformation. You will look back on your teen years as a cycle of the past, just as you now look back on your childhood as a past cycle. New growth and learning is the way of the Phoenix. Those born in Phoenix years are exacting, intelligent, and take pride in work well done.

They can succeed greatly in life by using their keen judgment, quick wit, and creative flair. They can overcome obstacles and create opportunities for new beginnings. Sometimes Phoenix is translated as Rooster or Cock. But you are only a Rooster or Cock if you peck and fight with others, always want your own way, or are fussy and controlling.

Phoenix Tale

The rare and enticing Phoenix is a universal symbol of transformation, rebirth, and eternity. The Phoenix rose anew from the flames of purification and was not destroyed. In China the Phoenix is honored as a symbol of the Empress, the earth, and feminine yin energy. A Phoenix on a woman's wedding dress shows that she is Empress for a day. As a symbol of marriage, the noble Phoenix is partnered with Dragon, a symbol of the Emperor. There is a very ancient tale of a cinnabar red Phoenix who was born in Southern China and who represents fire and summer. Cinnabar is a substance used in Taoist alchemy and magic, so this magical bird also denotes female genitalia in sex magic. Another tale tells of three Phoenixes. Children ride on their backs and carry vases filled with peonies, the queen of Chinese flowers. Peonies also symbolize female genitalia. Peonies attract butterflies, another reference to sexual coupling.

Phoenix Friends and Foes

Phoenixes together are not always compatible. All the other Chinese astrology signs are compatible with those born in the same year. But two Phoenixes sometimes fight and peck. Within a flock of Phoenixes there can be clashing and competitiveness. This is because Phoenixes are independent and proud. They do not want to bend to the will of others. Phoenix is most compatible with those born in the year of the Ox and Serpent. Phoenix also admires the power and majesty of Dragon. Dragon and Phoenix together are a traditional Chinese symbol of marriage. Phoenix is least compatible with Hare, Phoenix's opposite. Hare years are not lucky for Phoenix. Instead, Phoenixes are lucky in Ox, Dragon, Serpent, and Phoenix years. These lucky years are best for marriage or having a child. Select a pet born in one of these years to be harmonious with your animal.

Phoenix Life Areas

Teen life choice area for thrifty Phoenix should emphasis the Wealth area. Acquiring, spending, and investing money offers Phoenix a sense of security and power. Once Phoenix feels secure, they can make a powerful contribution to humanity as leaders and innovators. Because Phoenix's eccentric personality often clashes with others, embellishment of the Relationships/Romance area helps ease the path to harmonious interactions, especially with classmates.

Teen Dog

The Dog is a very valued animal in traditional China. Dogs are famous for their exceptional loyalty to family and profound aggressiveness with strangers. These behavioral extremes are manifestations of yin and yang. Dog is yin when faithful, devoted, and relaxed at home playing with children. Dog is yang when a fierce guardian, suddenly barking and growling at strangers. Just like a real Dog, a person born on Dog year can be loyal and kind—or aggressive and strong—depending on their circumstances. But Dogs are great people! They are candid, generous, fair, smart, and possess integrity of character. They care about the underdog and work for the betterment of all humanity. A classroom of Dogs is studious and energetic. They are also good athletes with many natural talents and abilities.

Dog Tale

There are many Chinese tales that demonstrate the loyalty and intelligence of Dogs. According to one tale, a farmer accidentally fell into a well. His Dog wondered why the farmer did not return home that evening, sniffed him out, and howled by the side of the well. A passerby heard the Dog's howling. He approached the well and shouted down to the farmer that he would help get him out of the well. But the passerby was so impressed with the loyalty of the Dog that he insisted that the farmer give him the Dog in exchange for being rescued. The farmer was upset because he loved his Dog and did not want to lose him, but he needed to get out of the well. Suddenly the Dog stuck his head into the well, as if reassuring the poor farmer. The passerby helped the farmer out of the well and left with the Dog. The Dog returned to the farm the next day.

Dog Friends and Foes

Dog is very compatible with other Dogs, like dogs in a pack. Dog is also compatible with those born in the year of the Tiger and Horse. Dog, Tiger, and Horse are dynamic, adventuresome, athletic, and free spirited. Dog cherishes the peace and gentility offered by Hare that helps Dog become calm. Dog is least compatible with Dragon, Dog's opposite. Dragon years are not lucky for Dog. Instead, Dog is lucky in Tiger, Hare, Dragon, and Dog years. These lucky years are best for marriage or having a child. Select a pet born in one of these years to be harmonious with your animal.

Dog Life Areas

Teen life choice area for Dog should emphasize the Career gua because Dogs believe passionately in what they do. If a Dog is compromised in his career choice, he suffers until this is corrected. Also of importance for Dog is the Family/Health area that inspires Dog's sense of loyalty and duty. Teen

Dogs usually mature early, and must be aware that they do not unfairly shoulder heavy family responsibilities or become too serious about family matters.

Teen Boar

 Don't be upset to read that you are born in the year of the Boar (also translated as Pig). You are not a slob, nor are you boring. Boars are lovable, easygoing, artistic, kind, and honest. They make great friends due to their generosity, heart-felt spirit, and their ability to forgive others. Boars are sturdy, strong, and often good at endurance sports such as hiking. Once a Boar sets a goal, they can be very determined to follow through and will not hurt or use others in the process. They usually have good taste and a flair for fashion. But teen Boars must not be overly indulgent with food, drink, excessive partying, or drugs. Be aware to not develop addictive behavior.

Boar Tale

A classic Chinese tale tells of a smart Boar who refused to work for the farmer who owned him. All the other animals labored: Ox plowed the field, Cat chased away Rat, Horse pulled a cart, Monkey carried the farmer's son to school on Monkey's back, Rooster crowed at dawn and hens produced eggs, and Dog kept guard. But Boar just ate and slept and ate and slept. Boar even complained about the quality of his food. He declared that he would have food whether or not he worked, so why bother to contribute? When Boar least expected it, the farmer sold him and his life of ease and contentment ended.

Boar Friends and Foes

Teen Boar is most compatible with those born in the year of the Hare and Sheep, who are also artistic and generous souls. Boar is compatible with another Boar and loves the wild Tiger, who inspires Boar and helps Boar when stuck with a problem or when doubtful of which way to proceed. Boar is least compatible with Serpent, Boar's opposite. Good-natured Boar may not always relate well to the intense and complex Serpent. Serpent years are not lucky for Boar. Instead, Boar is lucky in Hare, Tiger, Sheep, and Boar years. These lucky years are best for marriage or having a child. Select a pet born in one of these years to be harmonious with your animal.

Boar Life Areas

Teen life choice area for kindhearted and gullible Boar should emphasize the Helpful people/Travel area so that Boar can find support from others and not be taken advantage of. Boar should also emphasize the Relationships/Romance area to create a special intimate circle of kind partners, friends, family, and coworkers who will cherish Boar. Sometimes Boars can be indulgent when moderation is required, so cleaning up and overall balance of all eight areas is helpful.

A Feng Shui Makeover

feng shui makeover can completely transform the chi of your room and your life. You've learned the many different aspects of feng shui: yin, yang, sha chi, the eight guas, the five elements, and feng shui cures. Hopefully you can now pull all of these concepts together to give yourself and your friends a feng shui makeover. To give you an idea of how simple a feng shui makeover can be once you understand the basics, here is what sixteen-year-old Honora did to makeover her room.

Honora's feng shui makeover was tailored to her personality and her goals. Honora's primary passions are art and design. She plans to have a career in that field. She keeps busy with many creative projects and has a lot of friends. Having a romantic relationship is not a huge priority for her at this time in her life. She receives a small allowance from her parents each month and does odd jobs, like working at a local jazz festival, to supplement her income. She wants a more steady job in the next year to help pay for college. Honora generally gets along well with her parents who support her in her creativity and encourage her art by giving her opportunities to visit different art programs and museums.

The primary goal for Honora's makeover was to focus on the Creativity/Children gua. Basic feng shui balance in the other guas of the room assisted in the positive flow of chi that helped her to achieve her goals.

The critical issue in Honora's room was that it was the room she had since she was a little girl. Her environment didn't reflect who Honora is now at age sixteen. She had been sleeping on the bottom bunk of a set of bunk beds that her father had made for her when she was a child. The top bunk was full of clutter: books, blankets, makeup, magazines, and more. It was definitely time for a larger, more adult bed with plenty of space. She would not be limited by the boundary of a top bunk or clutter. Honora's parents were very supportive of her feng shui makeover. They removed the bunk bed and purchased a new, adult bed for Honora. If buying a new bed had not been an option financially, Honora could have taken down the upper bunk and kept only the lower bunk to use as her bed.

The element Earth is strong in Honora's personality, so she has the tendency to be like a pack rat and gather clutter. This can slow down her creative projects. When Honora sat and went through the items that were causing the majority of the clutter, she found that many of them were things she no longer had any use for. Most of them were left over from her childhood, such as dolls, doll clothes, and childhood books. She had maps of the world that she had memorized in grammar school and no longer needed. She was eager to give away her childhood belongings.

Honora went through her closet and wooden chest and got rid of clothes that no longer fit. She recycled some old fashion magazines and took down a poster of Albert Einstein that had interested her as a kid but no longer suited her now that she was older. When she was done, Honora was amazed by how much more space was in her room.

The few remaining bits of clutter went in their appropriate designated spots. Loose books went on the bookshelf, art supplies got tucked away into drawers, and clothes were folded and put away. With the big bunk bed gone and the room clutter-free, Honora finally had an open canvas to work with. Honora and her mother took the opportunity to paint the room. She chose a soft light yellow that was beautiful. This corresponds to the element Earth, so she had a natural affinity for this color. After receiving a fresh coat of paint, Honora's room seemed like a completely different space. It's amazing how the energy of a room transforms drastically for the better with a fresh coat of paint.

Once the paint dried, Honora and her mom brought in the new bed. Honora's old bed had been in the Helpful people/Travel gua, which would be appropriate for a young child in the years when parents and teachers play such a critical role in their development. As a young adult, however, Honora would benefit greatly from having her bed in the commanding position, which would heighten her independence. In Honora's case, placing the bed in the commanding position was even more beneficial because this was her Creativity/Children gua. She and her mom placed the bed in the commanding position so that it faced the mouth of chi in the Knowledge gua. The new bed was placed in the center of the wall, so that Honora could easily see the door from the bed without being in direct line of entry into the room. She anchored the balance of her bed by placing matching night stands, which she had painted herself, on both sides of the bed. But her new bed didn't have a headboard. A headboard is important to add stability and protection during sleep, so Honora created a headboard effect by hanging three pillows on hooks where a headboard would be. This looked great and gave the feeling of a thick, comfy headboard.

Honora decided to hang a soft pink and white painting that she liked over the center of her bed. She had a great collections of funky purses that she previously hung grouped together on a wall in her Fame/Reputation gua but took up too much space on the wall. She made use of the high ceilings in her room to hang her funky purse collection symmetrically along the top of the far walls, creating a nice border decoration while freeing up her Fame/Reputation gua wall space. Purses cover the guas of Relationships/Romance, Creativity/Children, and Helpful people/Travel. This added lively fun chi to all three of these areas.

Honora has a window in her Fame/Reputation gua. Before this was dressed with dark green drapes that made the room feel dark and small. The dark drapes created a bit of sha chi around the window area. She replaced this with beautiful sheer pink drapes that perfectly expressed the element Fire and enhanced her fame and reputation as a creative person and a great friend.

The cluttered dresser with a mirror above it that had previously been in the Wealth corner was moved and centered against the wall in the Family/Health area. It is best to get any sort of mirror out of the Wealth gua because no teen saving for college needs money reflected away from their pockets. The dresser was cleaned, the drawer contents organized, and clutter was removed from the dresser top. The water element of the mirror worked well to nurture the Wood element of the wooden dresser, giving the Family/Health area a nice, nurturing feel.

Honora moved her bookcase into the Helpful people/Travel area of her room, which is appropriate because books can help you to learn. The initial concern was that the bookcase might be too close to the bed, overpowering the sleeper. Once the new bed was in place it became clear, however, that there was plenty of space. Honora has a closet in her Career gua which is an asset because it adds extra chi to an area that she will be developing over the next few years. It will be very important that she keeps the closet uncluttered or she might begin to experience setbacks in her career. Honora placed a dressing mirror on the closet door, which is perfect because mirrors embody water and Career is associated with the Water element. Then she hung a large blank piece of paper next to the closet door. She decorated the paper with words and personal graffiti. This is totally appropriate because she is seeking a profession in the arts. It was also a great way to express herself and change the paper when she wants a new clean canvas for writing and journaling.

The entry to Honora's bedroom is located in the Knowledge area. This area receives energy every time she enters and exits her room. But her door was squeaky, generating sha chi every time the door opened. She oiled the hinges of the door with olive oil. Honora made sure the doorway could easily be kept clean and uncluttered. She put her jewelry collection behind the door, hung on a mesh net. The door can still open freely, but when it's shut one can view the decorative jewelry from the bed. The jewelry's sparkle gives good energy to her Knowledge area of life. It's fine to have collections, such as Honora's purses or jewelry. Collections should always be well organized and placed according to feng shui principles. If your collection gets too large, edit it down to the best pieces.

The final touch to Honora's makeover was the lighting. Her room was large and had natural light from the big windows in the Fame/Reputation area. But the room seemed dingy at night due to the overhead lighting. Honora had one overhead fixture that didn't have a cover and was powered by one high wattage bulb. The simple, inexpensive investment in a paper lantern cover completely transformed the lighting of the room from a stark, prisonlike glare to a bright yet soft glow that softened the feel of the room. This new soft lighting allowed one to see freely yet the soft light still offered peaceful yin energy.

The feng shui makeover had a very positive effect on Honora's life. She takes pride in her room, likes to keep it clean and organized, and loves spending time there. Most important for Honora, she now has an age appropriate space. She no longer lives in a little girl's room with bunk beds and stuffed animals.

17

Beyond Your Room

Now that you have successfully designed your room, consider how you can extend your knowledge into the world. Feng shui is typically applied to an entire house, with each room finding it's place in a particular gua. Each room is influenced by the gua in which it is located.

Applying the ba-gua chart to the whole house is the same as applying it to your room—the guas are determined by the mouth of chi.

Determining the Mouth of Chi in a House or Apartment

You can figure out how the eight areas of life apply to your family's living space by aligning it with the main entrance of the house or apartment. If you live in a place that has two or more floors, the mouth of chi of the upper floors is determined by the staircase. If there is more than one staircase, the mouth of chi is based on the one that receives the most use.

If you live in an apartment building, you can figure out what gua your specific apartment is in by considering the main entrance of the building as the mouth of chi. Your ba-gua map is still applied to the apartment layout by using the main door of your apartment as the mouth of chi. Individual rooms use their own entrance as the mouth of chi to align the ba-gua map.

Living Room: Yang, Fire

The living room is associated with Fire, the most yang of all the elements. This makes the living room the most exciting place of the house. Have you ever noticed how people will congregate around a campfire, fireplace, or woodstove? Fire attracts social behavior while offering a sense of warmth and security. Ideally, the living room should be placed next to the entryway. This is the first room a guest experiences and it can attract new people or repel them, depending on the health of the chi. Positive chi in a living room can be especially encouraged with live flowering plants or a seating area in the Wealth gua, with soft curtains or shades that encourage a sense of security while allowing for a well-lit room. The furniture of the living room should be facing the mouth of chi.

Dining Room: Yin, Earth

The yin dining room is in contrast to the yang living room. Calming yin energy should be cultivated to keep eaters relaxed and wanting to linger after the meal. It's unfortunate that so many schools employ very yang flourescent lighting and harsh furniture against stone or tile floors for their cafeterias. Televisions should not go in this room. Round or oval tables are more preferable because they are more yin then square ones. Soft lighting, muted colors, gently curved furniture, and rugs greatly enhance the yin of this room. Comfort is key. Candles are perfect lighting and music should be soft and soothing. Wherever possible, avoid sitting at any dining table where your chair faces a corner edge of a square or rectangular table. The corner point directed at your stomach can cause indigestion.

Bathrooms: Yin, Water

We cleanse, bathe, and purify in the bathroom. It must be kept clean. It's important to always keep the toilet seat down when you are finished with it, and to make sure none of your drains are clogged. A blocked drain affects your money because money is symbolized by Water in feng shui. Watch out for too much clutter with grooming products. Too much makeup is another way to create bathroom clutter. Soothing items work well in a bathroom: yin incense, candles, bath salts, and nurturing products.

Kitchen: Yang, Wood

Cleanliness in the kitchen is crucial because here is where food is prepared. White is a wonderful kitchen color because it enhances the sense of order. Green also works well as an accent color because green represents the element Wood. Healthy plants in the kitchen are good. Ideally the stove should be in the commanding position, though few of us have the opportunity to move the stove around. If your bedroom shares a wall with your kitchen make sure that the headboard of your bed is not back-to-back with your stove. Otherwise, your sleep will be distracted by the yang energy of the stove. You also don't want your head to be sharing a wall with a toilet or refrigerator. A stove in the Fire (Fame/Reputation) gua of the kitchen might create a little too much chi and lend toward a tendency for accidental fire. While you may not have any control over where things are placed in the kitchen or how it is decorated, there is one thing that almost anyone can negotiate in their household: don't keep the trash in the Relationships/ Romance gua of the kitchen. This can create problems with friends, family, and romance. Empty the trash daily to remove the smell and consequences of sha chi. Regardless of what your family thinks about your feng shui ideas, few parents will try to convince you that extra help around the house won't improve your relationships.

Other Rooms

For other rooms in the house, such as an office or den, it is important to mix yin and yang energy. If there is a central piece of furniture accenting the focal point of that room—such as a desk in the office or a couch in the den—it is ideal to place this furniture in the commanding position.

ACTIVITY: APPLY THE BA-GUA TO YOUR HOUSE

Map out the feng shui of your entire house or apartment. In what gua or guas are the following living spaces:

Where is the mouth of chi to your home?_____

Kitchen: _____

Living room: _____

Dining room: _____

Master bedroom: _____

Your bedroom: _____

Additional bedrooms: _____

Can you locate the mouth of chi in each room and align it to the ba-gua map?

Sustaining Harmony

Now that you have put all that work into arranging your room how do you maintain the positive chi? Once you've achieved a satisfactory sense of balance in your room, you can nourish your feng shui lifestyle by developing habits that support your everyday living activities without introducing clutter or disharmony. If you're having a hard time fending off the buildup of clutter, then perhaps your room needs to be reorganized.

- ☯ **Closets:** Do you avoid hanging up clothes? What are your hangers like? Do clothes fall off them all the time because they are too small, too wiry, or too crowded? Find a style of hanger that you enjoy and invest in filling your closet with matching hangers of that style. If you have space, consider screwing hooks into the inside of your closet in order to hang the items that you use frequently but that don't fit well on a hanger.

- ☯ **Trash:** Are you emptying it frequently enough, or is it overflowing in such a way that you end up throwing things on the floor or keep possessions that you would otherwise throw away? Are you keeping it *full* enough—tossing out useless mail and other objects as they come in rather than holding on to them for no particular reason? Create a schedule for yourself so that on the same day of every week you get in the habit of emptying the trash, no matter how full or empty it is. If you live in a community where trash is picked up once a week instead of every day, try to coordinate your trash emptying day so that it is the day before garbage pick-up. Examine all pieces of mail and any new items before they enter your room. Dispose of junk mail immediately. If you have a magazine subscription, remember to get rid of one old magazine every time you bring a new one in.

- ☯ **Recycling:** Do you end up storing bottles, cans, and paper because you haven't figured out what gets recycled or how frequently it gets recycled? Make sure you have a solid recycling bin for each kind of recyclable. If there is no recycling in your building, find out how to get started.

- ☯ **Misplaced items:** Do you have items that you intentionally placed in one gua but they keep wandering over to another, and another, and another? It's most likely a sign that you are not using that item consciously. Pay extra special attention to that item. Has it been placed properly? Do you need to establish a special location for it—such as a hook for your keys or backpack? After a few weeks of conscious item placement you will discover that the new habit of proper placement has become second nature.

- ☯ **Drawers:** Can you find the clothes you are looking for when you want them? Keep like articles of clothing together, such as T-shirts in top drawer and jeans in the bottom drawer. Keep all underwear in the same place, all shoes together, and so forth.

- ☯ **Laundry:** Do recently worn clothes end up creatively draped around your room instead of in a hamper? If the clothes are dirty, put them in a hamper. Otherwise, the chaos they create will hamper you. If you want to use them again, even though they have been worn once or twice, then store them with your clean clothes.

- ☯ **Papers:** Do papers end up sprawled all over your flat surface spaces, rather than in notebooks, files, or accessible, organized storage bins? Consider a filing system. It doesn't matter what logic the filing system uses as long as the logic meets your needs of being able to find what you want, when you want it.

- ☯ **CDs, tapes, DVDs:** Do CDs and the like end up lying around your room? If you haven't already located a place for all of your CDs then do so. The Creativity/Children gua is best. If you have a hard time putting CDs back, use a portfolio where the CDs slip in and out with ease.

Introduce New Items with Care . . .

Perhaps the most important key to retaining balance in your new room is to introduce new items consciously and with care. If your new item means that you are replacing an old item, then that old item may become clutter and must be removed. Consider your intention with new items—as well as their color, material, and shape—and consciously assign them a proper place in your room and in your life.

Feng shui is a lifelong journey. Now that you know how to apply this knowledge, keep it alive. Keep creating and attracting your own good luck.

BOOKS OF RELATED INTEREST

I CHING FOR TEENS
Take Charge of Your Destiny with the Ancient Chinese Oracle
by Julie Tallard Johnson

THE THUNDERING YEARS
Rituals and Sacred Wisdom for Teens
by Julie Tallard Johnson

TEEN ASTROLOGY
The Ultimate Guide to Making Your Life Your Own
by M. J. Abadie

TAROT FOR TEENS
by M. J. Abadie

THE GODDESS IN EVERY GIRL
Develop Your Teen Feminine Power
by M. J. Abadie

TEEN DREAM POWER
Unlock the Meaning of Your Dreams
by M. J. Abadie

FENG SHUI FOR LIFE
Mastering the Dynamics between Your Inner World and Outside Environment
by Jon Sandifer

TAOIST FENG SHUI
The Ancient Roots of the Chinese Art of Placement
by Susan Levitt

INNER TRADITIONS • BEAR & COMPANY
P.O. Box 388 • Rochester, VT 05767 • 1-800-246-8648
www.InnerTraditions.com

Or contact your local bookseller